Out Of The Shadow
I Can and I Will

Darol Rodrock

Lovingly transcribed and written by Paige Grauer Deruyscher

ISBN-13: 978-1977683380

ISBN-10: 197768338X

"No one can read this tale of Darol's remarkable journey without being greatly impacted on many levels. From a childhood few of us can imagine to a successful business and community leader, his story, insights, and spiritual awakening will challenge and inspire you in all facets of your life."
— Mike Vineyard, Retired CEO, Cramer Products, Inc.

"Hearing Darol talk to the students in our foundation's 'C' You at the 'K' program, it's obvious he has not only a remarkable story, but an incredible heart for people. Every time I hear Darol speak or spend time with him, I'm inspired to give more of myself to others. Now we're all blessed with the opportunity to read his inspirational story."
— Dayton Moore, General Manager, Kansas City Royals;
Founder, "C" You In The Major Leagues Foundation

"Darol Rodrock's journey is not unlike that of a diamond. Out of the dirt and darkness, through pressure and pain, he emerged strong and brilliant, shining in his truth. Darol loves sharing his mottos with men, women, and children so they, too, can overcome their feelings of despair, hopelessness, and loneliness that Darol once felt as a youth. No matter what your circumstances are, Darol offers inspiration, insight, and a unique viewpoint that shines brightly into even the darkest of shadows."
— Bobbi Jo Reed, Executive Director at the Healing House

If this book moves your heart in such a way you feel compelled to help with my mission, please consider donating to the Darol Rodrock Foundation at: www. darolrodrockfoundation.org.

Table of Contents

FOREWORD

Early in my career, I became aware of a successful real estate up-and-comer who was working as both a builder and developer, while simultaneously teaching and coaching successful high-school wrestling teams. Needless to say, I was impressed! It's not often you encounter someone so industrious and hard-working.

Darol Rodrock's name quickly grew in the industry. Soon, he became so successful he had to focus solely on building and developing. And how he went about creating a community was a sight to behold!

I observed and admired the tenacity and strategy with which Darol created his neighborhoods. Every element had such forethought, including immediately selling land to the school district so that the communities had nearby schools! Beautiful, welcoming entry monuments and pools appeared at once. There were playgrounds, plenty of green space, and paved trails that beckoned families to come outside and take a walk. Yet most importantly, Moms'

Councils were created to provide unique, family-oriented opportunities. From holiday parties to bike parades and more, these gatherings helped bestow an immediate sense of community, especially for families moving in from out of town. Darol seemed to honestly care about the communities he was creating—and each individual family that built within his neighborhoods.

It became readily apparent that Darol approached business as it was done decades ago. In other words, he did everything with the utmost attention to doing things the right way. For Darol, people came first. And profit? That came far down the line. To this day, Darol Rodrock is one of the most respected names in the residential real-estate business. He's not only survived—but *thrived*—for more than three decades, even when recessions hit and the economy took downturns. Darol stands behind what he does and handles business matters with absolute integrity. I can attest, after more than 35 years in the real-estate industry, this is rare, indeed.

As our paths continued to cross professionally—I loved to sell in Darol's communities; there was a spirit of cooperation par excellence—I began to unearth more about his past. He really had come from nothing, your classic American Dream come true. There was nothing assuming or entitled about Darol's character.

He treated the bulldozer operator with the same respect he granted the bank president. Darol had an uncanny way of immediately putting everyone and anyone at ease and of speaking to each individual as if they were the sole focus of his attention.

Once, I invited him to speak to a group of our top-performing agents. As Darol answered questions regarding business and real estate, he remained attentive and professional. Yet when I asked questions tapping into his past, I was shocked to see Darol moved to tears.

Darol's happy-go-lucky demeanor crumbled as he opened up about a most unspeakable past. We were left speechless. So often, when we see highly successful individuals, we assume they were raised in a happy family environment, where all things were wonderful and easy. It was absolutely jolting to see how a devastating past filled with abandonment and poverty had given way to a thriving career. After all, Darol was the number-one developer in Johnson County, the most affluent county in the entire state of Kansas. He owned vacation homes, horses, and boats. Darol was highly respected among his peers and generous to a fault. This revelation led me to say, "Darol, your story MUST be told!!!"

We met for breakfast shortly after, and Darol sat down and said, "You know, when I learned there was this little Jewish man named Jesus who would love me no matter what. He became my friend for life..." And on his story went, his tale of survival, his success at leaving the shadow of his past behind. I was mesmerized.

So I invite you, encourage you, challenge you, to read this book and be inspired by "Little Darol," who with his grit, determination, and sheer creative courage brings you to the brilliant conclusion that *anyone* can be *anything*, can overcome seemingly insurmountable obstacles, and, most importantly, survive and thrive!

Be blessed and inspired by this book—and share! Come to love Darol as a good friend, like so many others have done. And take his message into your heart, so you can leave whatever hinders you in the past. Leave all that darkness behind you, shine in the light of your own truth, and reach out to help others in need. I tell you, Darol has shown us that such an act of courage can be absolutely life changing.

—*Judy Johns*
Owner, Keller Williams Realty Partner

PREFACE

For years I've been encouraged to write down my story. Those I've shared it with have found it inspiring and, in some cases, even life changing. I've learned that the more I reveal what I've been through, the more others are able to open up about their own lives. It's a healing thing for a person to feel truly understood for the first time and to discover they aren't alone on the journey, no matter what challenges they may face.

But this story, this most personal of biographies, was hard for me to tell. It brings to light many of the horrors I endured as a little boy. And I've been afraid to make myself vulnerable. Will it be too painful to remember? How will people respond? Will they believe me? Will I offend my family, whom I dearly love? It's something that I grappled with deeply for more than a decade.

I have come to a place of understanding my own journey. In turn, it's helped me understand the journey of my parents and siblings—all from a vantage point of compassion. I am grateful for my family, despite all the dysfunction, because each member, in their own way, taught me tenacity and drove me to do better with myself, and to do so without judgment. Each of us found our own paths in life, some with more success than others.

Through the years, I've come to realize that all that happened to me—the violent blows, cruel acts and words—formed the darkest of shadows over me. And even as a young boy I somehow understood I had two choices: I could live under this shadow for the rest of my life, or I could leave it behind me and step into the glorious light of freedom.

What you hold in your hands is my story of survival and the beliefs that helped me not only endure, but triumph over my past. This book is for anyone who's looking for real and lasting hope. No matter who you are, what your past was, or what you're going through now, I want to inspire you with this thought: *You can overcome anything life brings.*

In these pages, I offer some insight into how an abused, abandoned, and afraid little boy grew into a man who's found a life of purpose and joy. This is the story of how I learned to accept the past for what it was, let the future be what it will be, and live more fully and freely in the present.

This book is filled with things I need to remind

myself of day after day. It's not for preaching to you, telling you what to believe, or suggesting how you should live. It's about the hope I've discovered in my life, the strength I've found within myself, and the encouraging words that keep me going. There are truths here that I've spoken to my own heart so many times they've become a part of me. And while my "sermons" are for me, if they can inspire even one person on their own journey, then my story will be worth telling.

If I've learned anything in my 70-plus years, it's that our lives are made up of choices. Moment by moment, we are choosing our life experience, whether we're aware of it or not. We can allow our circumstances to define us, we can listen to other people tell us who we are, and let the world decide what we can and cannot do...*or* we can choose to live the lives *we* want to live—the kind filled with purpose, peace, and love.

Through the abuse and abandonment of my childhood and the challenges of growing up in foster care, I faced this decision many times: Would I give up and give in to bitterness, become a victim of what life had given me? Would I give in to anger and despair? Or would I find a way to keep going—to not just survive but thrive and be blessed every day of my life?

Please know that writing this book *isn't* about me

having all the answers. It's not me saying, "I finally got it! I've overcome it all. So now let me show *you* how to do it." No, I'm saying that this is the way I cope with my own life—*every day*—and move forward.

I can't offer you the answers for your life. Those are yours alone to discover. But what I *can* do is share *my* truths—the things that helped me through—that *still* get me out of bed every day. Perhaps something in my story will speak to you, right where you are in your own life. Or maybe you'll be inspired to help others on *their* journey.

You see, I believe the difference between making it and not making it in life is sometimes a very small step. If I can help someone take steps *away* from despair and *toward* feeling pride in themselves, then I'll share my message with anyone I can reach.

But it's not an easy message to share. It's a collection of memories filled with a great deal of ugliness—and some of my memories aren't shared here, because they're too graphic for print. For this reason, and so many others, it's a history that almost remained buried.

But then one day my good friend, Dave, told me a tale that finally convinced me that perhaps I should be sharing mine.

Dave entered the U.S. Army when he was 19. He was going through basic training in Georgia in the sweltering heat of summer, 104 degrees, marching for miles with a 100-pound pack on his back.

There was a moment when Dave decided he just couldn't make it anymore. Exhausted and ready to faint, he was just about to say, "I quit! I can't do it."

Suddenly, this big, tall, 6'4" gangly lookin' guy standing close to him started singing, "I'm gonna make it...I'm gonna make it...I'm GONNA MAKE IT!"

Something happened for my friend in that moment. He was inspired! He said to himself, "If that sucker can make it, then I can, too!"

So he started singing, and pretty soon the whole platoon was singing along, "We're gonna make it...we're gonna make it!"

Dave told me, "I often wonder how it would've affected my life had I quit the Army that day. Something like that stays on your record forever. Would I have had the same opportunities? The same accomplishments? Would I have been the president of a bank or would my journey have taken a totally different turn? I know one thing. My life was changed by one, tall, skinny guy who started singing!"

Hearing that story made me realize it's time for me to start singing. I am grateful for the friends who've encouraged me to do so. It's time for me to get out of my own way and let people hear, "We're gonna make it!"

I realize, now more than ever, how much we need to inspire one another along the journey. My story would've had a very different outcome if it were not for the grace of God and the people who opened their arms and hearts to me, a struggling boy who just needed to know his worth, his purpose, and his potential.

I want to help the next little girl or boy on the path, and I'm inviting you to join me. In my story, you may find a little bit of yourself somewhere—in the child struggling to make sense of his own life, or maybe in the people who saw his need and welcomed him into their hearts.

If one man, woman, or child can say, "I can hear him singing! I'm gonna make it, too!" then I believe my story will be worth telling.

—*Darol Rodrock*

I CAN AND I WILL

Darol, age 5, in Iola, Kan., with one of his only toys,
a bike tire.

1

LITTLE DAROL

How my journey began

There are moments of my childhood that are burned into my memory—pictures I can still see so vividly when I close my eyes. I can hear the shuffling, panic, and screaming from the night we were bitten by rats that had infested our home. We were huddled together, four young children and our mother, living in a small, two-room shack called Looker's Cabins in Iola, Kan., where there was little food or comfort to be found.

We were terrified of those big, long-tailed rats. They'd come in one corner of the room up through holes in the floor, run behind the divan, and go out the other corner. Vermin that usually stuck to the shadows climbed onto the thin mattress my family shared and sunk their teeth into my arm and my mother's neck, drawing blood. It was a terrifying moment for a 4-year-old boy. The ambulance and police cars came; we were rushed to the hospital and given rabies shots. What I remember even more than the painful bites was my mother's shrieks and hysteria.

I have so many memories like this one—glimpses of the hard times that shaped my childhood years. But like every life, there are stories behind my story, so that's where I'll begin...

My mother, Maxine Thomas, was born in Centerville, Kan., in 1923. She was raised on a farm— a pretty young thing with long, dark hair and blue eyes. She married my father, Whitford Rodrock, in 1940. Whitford worked in a Kansas oil field (like his father) before becoming a salesman later in life. He was a handsome man with a wide mouth and deep-set eyes—charismatic, a jokester with a lot of personality. But he had a terrible temper and eventually became a violent alcoholic, abusing his wife and children.

Whitford's father—my Grandpa Rodrock—hadn't set the best example. After leaving work in the oil fields, he became a bootlegger and was arrested for stealing cars. Whitford followed in his footsteps, leading a life of bootlegging, theft, and fraud.

Grandma and Grandpa Rodrock lost two children before Whitford was born, so I guess when he came along, he was *the one.* Grandma raised him to expect that he could do anything he wanted to. According to my mother, he beat every woman he was with and had no concern for anyone else. His explosive anger led him down a dead-end path, and he eventually served time in the Lansing, Kan., penitentiary.

Somehow, during the tumultuous years of their marriage, Whitford and Maxine had four beautiful children: Beverly, me, Donnie, and Barbara.

I made my entrance into the world on a snowy January night in an old farmhouse in a little town called Bush City in Anderson County, Kan. My Grandma Rodrock delivered me while Grandpa took two mules and a wagon to get the doctor 15 miles away in Garnett, Kan. There was a blizzard that day, and they didn't return until a week later. When the doctor finally did come, my birth certificate read: January 6, 1944. Grandma said, "No, Doctor! I delivered him at 10 o'clock in the morning on New Year's Day!"

My mother said my Grandma just wouldn't put me down. She held and loved me from the moment I was born. My mother got sick and was hospitalized soon after, and when she came home from the hospital,

Grandma *still* wouldn't give me to her! Here she was, this 5-foot, 100-pound little lady carrying me around until I was 2 years old. In fact, I was still lying across her lap like a baby when I was 4 with my feet dragging on the floor!

Even though I don't consciously remember those moments, I am grateful for them. I believe they were some of the only experiences of unconditional love and acceptance I had as a child. In a sense, my Grandma saved me. It was like what happens when someone imprints a colt. When a colt has a loving connection with a human being, he will grow up being unafraid of people. I am convinced that, without my Grandma's "imprint" I would have turned into a very different person.

Although my brother, sisters, and I each had our own experiences, I think there's no question that our shared childhood was very dysfunctional. We were often hungry and filthy. We went through years of terrible physical abuse and witnessed violent attacks between our parents that children should never see. Looking back, I'd have to say that evil things happened to us. There was so much pain; it's a struggle for me to describe it all today.

As I look back, I realize life was hard for my parents, too. My mother never finished high school and had no job skills. She started washing dishes for

$15 a week, and later worked as a waitress, along with whatever other jobs she could pick up. She was a young woman with few options, married to an abusive, alcoholic man. She had her first child at 17 and the rest of us soon after. Her own mother had died in her arms when she was a teenager, which must have been such a traumatic thing for a young girl. She never had the chance to learn how to be a mother herself. I've come to realize that her desperation just in surviving must have overwhelmed her.

Mother's need for male attention and affection sometimes clouded her view of her own kids. I think in her despair she'd turn her hurt and anger toward us—and I have to admit, it was mostly directed at me. Often, with no explanation, she would whip me brutally to blood.

My father was the very same way—angry, violent, and unpredictable. He was like striking a match. We'd be sitting there at the table talking and *POW* out of nowhere he'd smack someone as hard as he could with no warning. We lived in constant fear wondering what was to come next.

We spent the first years of our childhood in Iola, Kan., a small town southwest of Kansas City. We lived in a little two-bedroom house with one source of heat (a small gas stove) and an old outhouse for a bathroom. Our water came from a well.

We were young, but learning to survive on our own made us grow up fast. I remember our Uncle Ralph used to bring rabbits and squirrels for us to eat. He taught me to clean them when I was just 5 or 6 years old. Food was always scarce, and those squirrels and rabbits were always welcome. When my mother had flour or cornmeal, she would fry us mush as an after-school snack. It was sometimes all we had in the house.

Although my parents divorced when I was 4, my father showed up at the house from time to time throughout our childhood. One of my most vivid memories is one night, a few years later, he came home violently drunk and almost killed my little brother, Donnie. Whitford grabbed him and literally pounded his head on the floor until blood was running out of his ears, nose, and mouth. My sister, Beverly, my mother, and I did everything we could to stop him. We were terrified Donnie was dead. When his face turned blue, Whitford carried him to the sink and stuck his head under the coldwater faucet until Donnie started breathing again.

Whitford didn't like Donnie, because he was so much like my mother, Maxine, and beating Donnie was his way of unloading his anger and bitterness toward her. On the other hand, I was a lot like

Whitford, Maxine always said. And because she resented him so much, she took her anger out on me.

In the middle of the night, she'd wake me to bear the brunt of her bitterness and pain. I could hear her coming to the door, and I'd just lay there terrified. Sometimes she'd whip me so long I wondered if she'd ever stop. Then she'd cry, wipe the blood off, and tell me she loved me. It was so confusing. What did love mean? The beating? Or the "I'm sorry" afterward?

Relationships are hard for me. Even as an adult, I still carry the confusion from all those years ago. To this day, I have to sleep with my bedroom door locked as those old dreadful feelings sometimes haunt me. Even if the physical scars are gone, the fear is still very real. I think many abused children carry that anxiety and confusion with them the rest of their lives. It just takes a thought or a word to bring it all back to the surface.

Recently I recalled a story about sleepwalking when I was a child. I'd push a chair around at night in my sleep. Beverly remembers hearing it scrape across those old wood floors of our house in the dark. Guess even in my sleep I was trying to hide from Maxine. But Maxine heard me one night, and using her belt—a wide, Western belt with colored glass insets—she whipped me hard again. Beverly ran in and lay atop of me to protect me. Maxine beat her to blood for trying to help.

And it wasn't only physical abuse that defined those childhood years for us. It was total neglect. Poverty. No food. No heat. No care. Our homes were always cold, bare, and barren—never filled with any of the warmth and love that should accompany childhood memories.

At some point, we moved to Tennessee Street in Iola, a neglected, lonely little place—but with one bright spot every Christmas. Each year, the Salvation Army truck would arrive with the only gifts we could hope to receive. It was the highlight of our holiday. We never had the chance to believe in Santa. (In fact, Maxine once beat me brutally for waking her at the thought that I heard Santa!) Never even had a tree or anything. Mom didn't have $2 to her name. Her monthly welfare check was $50, and rent was $30, so we had only $20 to live on each month.

The year I turned 6, Donnie and I sat together on our front porch on Christmas Day, waiting anxiously for that big Salvation Army truck. It was getting dark, and they hadn't come. Donnie leaned toward me, and I put my arm around him. We just knew Christmas wouldn't happen that year. I'll never forget that hopeless, melancholy feeling in my little-boy heart. That one gift was all we had to look forward to at Christmas, and now it, too, was taken from us.

We'd pretty much given up when all of a sudden, the big truck rounded the corner and backed up in front of our house. Man, were we excited! They handed Donnie and me each a plastic red fire truck—a new toy of our very own! We took those trucks into the house, and being the boys that we were, we raced them around and ran them right into each other. Within 10 minutes, they were all broken up. And that was it. That was Christmas.

They were frightening times, too. We were cold, hungry, and frequently alone, left to take care of ourselves on many occasions. Often I'd run to the back door of the restaurant where Maxine was working, and she'd sneak me a bag of food she'd taken. That was our meal for the day.

It shouldn't have been hard to tell we were neglected at home, especially when it came to our personal hygiene. I wet the bed almost every night. We were too young to know what to do, and it seemed like we were never cleaned up. We'd go to bed each night, unable to find a dry spot. The smell alone was horrible. It got so bad that Donnie and I would take a blanket off the bed and climb down to the floor to sleep, but then that blanket would get wet, too! Nobody changed anything, washed anything. We didn't bathe, and we smelled all the time.

It was miserable. We all had toothaches and

earaches with no remedy but to lay with a hot water bottle near our faces. Donnie and I would cry and moan most of the night.

In second grade, my teacher told me to sit in the back of the room alone because of how awful I smelled. Can you imagine that kind of humiliation for a child? I remember the kids laughing and making fun of me. I was filled with anger. I wanted so much to sit in front with the others and just be normal. At one point, I was allowed to move up again. Then, we all got head lice, and it was right back to the back of the room...and an overwhelming sense of rejection.

Even though daily life was really rough, I was a pretty good kid—polite and respectful when I needed to be, but stubborn and strong-willed (which served me well in the toughest times). I always wanted to be liked, and my outgoing nature made me a natural leader of our little "homespun gang" from an early age. We little guys in East Iola formed small groups that fought each other with green-bean cans we'd hammered shut full of gravel and rocks. We threw them at each other like hand grenades. I was always the biggest and strongest of our group and knew how to stand up for myself so no one bullied me. It was a tough part of town, and I definitely ended up with what they call the "East Iola Mouth" (even today I call myself a white-collar redneck!).

Had it not been for my older sister, Beverly, just a child herself, I don't know what would've happened to me during those desperate years. She took care of us as best she could. I wonder how in the world she kept us going. Maxine would be gone for hours and hours or even days, and Beverly would try to feed us, clothe us—everything! I love her dearly, and as we've grown older, she's become one of my very best friends.

Beverly's sense of humor was something that kept us smiling, even in the poorest conditions. Near one of our homes in Iola, there was an acre of used tires stacked 10 feet high. We kids thought it was the perfect place to find adventure—our very own playground. (Never mind all the snakes and critters hiding in those tires!) There we were, little kids, jumping all over the place with no parents around, of course. One time Beverly dove down into one of those stacks of tires headfirst, and I was convinced she couldn't get out. It scared me to death. Beverly was my loving and supportive sister, and now she was the one crying for help. I had no idea she was teasing us, screaming, "HELP! HELP! HELP!" I ran up to the house calling for Maxine with all my might.

Years later, Maxine recalled that day. She said I tried everything I could—scratching, biting, kicking— to get her to come help Beverly. As we ran back to where she was supposedly stuck, we found her sitting atop the tires laughing hysterically. She has always loved to tease.

We had few possessions. My favorite toys were an old bicycle tire that I rolled everywhere with a stick and a small tin can that I would kick around for hours. Later, Uncle Ralph bought an old bicycle at a farm sale for a dollar. Of course, it never really worked and always had flat tires.

As I look back now, I can understand how even children living in the poorest of conditions need to find a way to laugh together and try to see the lighter side of life, especially when there's so much darkness at home. We certainly found ways to make our own fun, though it's a wonder we lived through some of the chances we took.

Without an adult around, we were pretty much free to do whatever we wanted. I was 6 and 7 years old when my buddies and I started riding trains for thrills. We'd go to the movies on Saturdays and then head down to the railroad yards. We started by just walking the tracks, but pretty soon, we were messing around on trains that were waiting in the yards. We'd climb the ladders onto boxcars to play in them. Then one day, one of the trains started moving, and we found ourselves riding all the way to the next stop. There were three towns all in a row: Iola, Humboldt, and Chanute. At first we were scared to death to be on those trains, but before we knew it, we had a regular route all the way to Chanute and back—32 miles round-trip! When the ride was over, we'd jump off, landing in big pits of sand by the tracks to break our fall.

Sometimes, we'd just go out and lay across the train tracks under a boxcar while the train was stopped, our heads on one side of the tracks, feet on the other. The last one to get up when the train started moving would win. The sound of that train moving along the tracks was unmistakable: Thunk...thunk...thunk. (And of course, I was the last one to come out every time, being the boy that I was! That stubbornness and fight would serve me well down the line.)

Another thing we'd do after a heavy rain is ride inner tubes down a storm-water project that was built in the '30s. It was about 5 feet wide and 4 feet deep and moved all the storm water from Iola to the river. It was nicknamed Coon Creek, because of all the raccoons that would come to pick up the trash and debris it carried. Under bridges, through culverts, the water was fast and furious and very dangerous. But that was exciting for a 6- and 7-year-old kid.

And because there was never enough money, I learned how to make a few pennies for myself. Looking back now, I can see that I was always pretty self-motivated, even as a child. If I wanted something, I knew I had to work to get it.

On Saturday mornings, I'd walk between Iola and Gas City and pick up glass pop bottles that had been thrown out along the road; they were worth 2 cents each when I turned them in at the store. The bottles couldn't be chipped at all, and I remember how hard it was to find that kind! I'd finally get five of them and take them back to Mr. Jones at the store, and he'd pay me. I needed 10 cents for the picture show.

One Saturday morning, my mother was particularly mean and angry toward me. I wanted to go to the movie that day, because Tom Mix was playing. (A few of you may remember who that was!) I thought I'd missed my chance, because I didn't have time to pick up pop bottles. But as I was walking by the store, I noticed the back gate to where Mr. Jones stored the bottles was open. I slipped in, took five out of the case, and just walked around to the front door. I said, "Mr. Jones, here are my pop bottles today!" He took them to the back and put them in the case.

As always, he patted me on the head, gave me my 10 cents and said, "See you next Saturday, Darol." I never picked up pop bottles again! I always wondered if he knew...

When I turned 7, I sold the *Grit* newspaper on the street corner next to a restaurant where Maxine worked. On a cold January day after school I stood there with my stocking cap pulled down, hoping to sell a few papers. I finally sold enough that I went in, bought some French fries, put them in my coat pocket, and took the ketchup bottle and poured it right into the pocket on top of the fries. Only thing I had to eat all day long.

Soon after, a man came by. I had eight newspapers left, and I sure hoped to sell him one. He made a rude remark, shoved past me, and turned the corner to the beer joint where my mother was working. I was freezing to death at the time. I followed him in and skinnied up to the bar beside him. He ordered a beer and threw $10 on the counter for my mother to make change. When he went to the restroom, I decided he needed to buy all my papers right then. So I took all the change. Likely, he might have paid too much for those newspapers! Of course when I got home that night, my mother took all the money—but I sure felt rich for a little while!

It was a feeling that was all too fleeting. Mother Nature was about to deliver a blow that even my ingenuity and grit couldn't save us from. The flood of 1951 was epic. It seemed like it flooded most everything from Oklahoma to Kansas City. We'd always had some flooding in our end of town, but that year, the water came up into the house. I remember my Grandpa Rodrock carrying us out of the house and into his car to escape the rising waters. When we returned home, we discovered that the floodwaters had reached the ceiling. We didn't have much to begin with, but now we'd lost even these small belongings. Our only possessions were the clothes on our backs!

Funnily enough, the thing I remember being saddest about were the two baby raccoons Uncle Ralph had given us. We fed them and played with them constantly. When they were washed away in the flood, we cried.

That was the turning point. The flood had left us in such a state that I think that's why the state welfare system interceded. One Saturday morning Miss West, a social worker who had visited us on a monthly basis for a couple of years, picked up the whole family in her '51 Chevy. It was two-door, black—I can see it perfectly in my mind to this day. We drove three hours from Iola to Winfield, Kan., and had no idea what was about to happen in our lives. She parked at the Lutheran Children's Orphanage, and we were all ushered in the door. There was a playroom with a TV, and we were enthralled. We'd never even seen a TV before! I remember my mother, arms and legs crossed, standing at the door. I looked back at the TV, looked up again...and she was gone.

That moment is indelibly burned into my mind. I

don't know if I loved her or not at that age. I was 7. She was my mother. She was all I had, all I knew. I saw that empty space where she'd been standing moments before and thought, "There's nobody at the door for me." I'm 73 years old today, and I can still remember thinking, "I can't believe Mom didn't say goodbye! There's nobody at the door. We never even got to say goodbye!"

I have often wondered how my mother must have felt in losing her children—she was just 27 years old. But looking back, being taken away was the greatest gift I could've been given, though I didn't know it at the time. All I thought was that I'd been abandoned and rejected, and I felt lonelier than ever in my life.

This was but the first of two times we were placed in the orphanage. We moved back and forth from Lutheran Children's to our mother's in the years that followed, until the state system evidently lost track of us.

Darol, Donnie, and Beverly in 1946.

Beverly and Darol in 1946.

Beverly, Darol, Donnie, Barbara—and Darol's favorite dog, Smokey, in 1952.

Whitford and Maxine, Darol's parents, about 1941.

OUT OF THE SHADOW

2

My Miss Pinnt

The difference one person can make

"Darol Rodrock, born January 1, 1944, is a nice looking boy. He cries easily, is very tender-hearted, is the least behavior problem of the four, likes praise and needs love and affection. He is sassy at times and they all use the same very bad words but are constantly among East Iola people that use this language all the time. [Darol] loves his mother, is loyal to her, and seldom mentions his father. He does fair work in school."

– Miss West, social worker

I was 7 years old the first time we were taken to

the orphanage. When the state returned us to our mother about a year and a half later, she'd had a hysterectomy and was suffering with some serious health problems after the surgery. Turns out, the doctor had made a mistake and left a sponge in her body. She almost died. Grandma Rodrock had stayed with us in Humboldt, Kan., during Maxine's surgery, but when complications arose, Grandpa Rodrock and our dad came to get us. They insisted we leave with them, but my sister Beverly held all of us kids back. A huge argument ensued, but we refused to go anywhere while our mother was in the hospital in such serious condition. We were terrified she was going to die, and there was no way we were going to leave.

A couple of years later, things again became so desperate at home that the state welfare system put us in the orphanage a second time. I was 10. As lonely and painful as it was, that time was another turning point for me because of one kind, compassionate soul who became a beacon of hope to a desperate Little Darol. In fact, I believe my story would have been a very different story if it hadn't been for this sweet lady who took the time to offer her love and care. While Charlotte Pinnt might have been young and small in stature, her impact on me was anything but. This quiet teacher at the Lutheran Children's School put her arm around me one day and told me something that changed my life.

Here's how it happened: When we lived at the orphanage, we attended church every Sunday. The front row was reserved for kids from the orphanage, so we always sat there, and we were always late. One Sunday, the Reverend Zehnder, a real flamboyant minister, looked at me during his sermon and said, "Jeeeeesus loves you!" I swear he looked me right in the eye.

I don't know why it hit me so powerfully in that moment—maybe because I was so desperate for that message. My brother and sisters were sitting next to me, but I don't think they were impacted like I was.

I went right home to Miss Minnie, the orphanage headmistress, and asked, "Who's this guy named Jesus? I want to meet Him!" Never heard the word "Jesus" or "love" where I came from.

Miss Minnie answered, "He's dead, and you can't meet Him."

I was crushed. I went back to the dormitory and cried all afternoon.

I'd heard about this Jesus who promised to always be with me after I'd felt abandoned for so long—Who loved me no matter what, after I'd felt so unlovable as a child. And now I could never know Him.

At school the next day, I decided I wasn't going to

give up on Jesus. I asked Miss Pinnt, my teacher, about Him. But she had a different answer. She put her arm around me and said, "He's alive, He does love you, and you can know Him."

Miss Pinnt was a darling young lady—kind, warm, and welcoming. Her open arms and loving spirit were all I needed to believe that there really was someone who loved me unconditionally. She made me feel the words she said were true, and that changed everything for me.

So I grew up with a guy named Jesus by my side. He became my best friend, and I imagined doing everything with Him. We played and explored and fished. He was there in the toughest times, when I was lonely, going through all those trials in my life. Even when I was feeling angry and hateful, mean and rejected, somehow I was reminded of what Miss Pinnt had taught me: that Jesus loves me.

There were times I thought I wasn't going to make it. Felt like I was falling off a cliff and reaching up and a little branch sticking out saved me from destruction. That was Jesus.

My favorite hymn today is "In the Garden." It touches me deeply to hear the words:
*"And He walks with me,
and He talks with me,
and He tells me I am his own..."*

Because that's what He has done all my life.

The best part of this story only came to light a few years ago. I had just begun to speak publicly about the difficulties I went through as a child. As I would tell about this caring lady, Miss Pinnt, who changed my life, I began to wonder what happened to her. *Where is she today? Is she still alive?* It had been more than 58 years since I'd left the orphanage.

So I made a few phone calls, and after a series of connections, a man on the other end of the line told me the good news: Yes she was there, and yes I could talk with her!

You can imagine the emotions that followed. First of all, I thought there was no way she'd remember who I was. But when I introduced myself, she said, "Yes, I remember you."

I said, "Well, that's awfully sweet, Miss Pinnt, but you don't need to say that to me."

She said, "Oh yes, I remember your little brother, Donnie, and little sister Barbara. Of course I remember you!"

I can't begin to describe the overwhelming sense of spiritual connection that happened in that moment for me. It was so fulfilling, just a tremendous wave of gratitude and surprise. It instantly brought me back to childhood—such a powerful, powerful feeling.

First of all, she remembered Little Darol, who is

still part of me. It just overwhelmed me, because that child had never been shown unconditional love and care until Miss Pinnt reached out to me all those years ago. Now here I was talking to the lady to whom I'd given so much credit for helping Little Darol along the road—and she actually remembered him, a little boy who'd felt so worthless and invisible. She even told me stories about him. I'd rarely had anybody in my life tell a story about me as a child. It was like putting missing pieces back together in my heart. I knew I had to see her.

I drove to her home in El Dorado, Kan., and met her again for the first time in more than five decades. Finally, I was able to thank her for all she had done for me, and I discovered she had no idea of the impact she'd made. Here's what she shared about her experience:

I loved teaching the kids from the orphanage in Winfield. It was so much fun because of the way they'd respond to the love and support we gave them. I think of how inexperienced I was, just fresh out of college. I know I must've overlooked a lot of things I should've done with those kids. What enormous problems some of them faced. I still feel guilty, because I believe I could've done a better job if I'd had more experience.

When Darol first contacted me, I was absolutely overwhelmed by his story, and by the fact that he remembered the things I'd said so many years ago. I couldn't even sleep for a couple of nights, wondering, "What has this boy turned into? Who is he?" I was puzzled about why he wanted to meet with me.

The day after he called, two of my own children who live in the Kansas City area came to visit, and I told them about a former student, named Darol Rodrock, contacting me. They actually knew who he was and couldn't believe that this well-known man had been in the orphanage so many years ago—and I had been his teacher!

The anticipation of his arrival was really neat for me. To this day, I am still so humbled to think of what a few words of love and encouragement meant to this boy almost 60 years ago. As I often remind Darol, it was God who put me in the right place at the right time and gave me the right words to say. And Darol's kindness toward me continues to this day. I still feel so unworthy of his gratitude. But I'm so thankful that God brought us together again after all these years!

Miss Pinnt introduced me to a story of love and hope, but even more than that, her actions showed me that that story was true.

And I needed that desperately at the orphanage. I knew I didn't want to leave and go back home, because I'd be beaten there. But there wasn't a lot of warmth to be found in this new, unfamiliar place. Miss

Minnie, the headmistress, was tough; she had to be! She was a nice lady but very stern. There was no family feeling there—just existence. No affection. No hugs. No "Good night, I love you."

I remember nights in the orphanage dormitory when my brother tried to crawl into bed with me. They'd make Donnie go back to his own bed, and he'd cry all night long. I tried to reach out with my little hand to hold his, but that wasn't allowed either. It was a terribly lonely, desperate existence.

But Miss Pinnt gave me a sense that there was something better—something more to life than always feeling abandoned and rejected. She helped me know we're never alone, even in life's darkest times. I want to give her credit for the love and kindness she showed. In fact, that's what she's done for me all my life. No matter where I find myself, I've always held on tight to what she gave me, and I still do to this day.

I don't know that the catechism book I studied did much for me (in fact, I still have the book to this day, and it still doesn't do much!). Rather it is hope and love that have made all the difference in my life.

And those are the gifts I try to pass on to people, whenever and however I can. If I can introduce them to this way of living I found in Jesus—a daily experience of His hope, love, and peace—then I've given them a gift that can last a lifetime. Long after I am gone, long after our paths have crossed, I know that I'm still making a difference in their lives...just like Miss Pinnt did in mine. I thank God for that special, special little lady!

Charlotte Pintt (now Charlotte Pintt Teuscher), 2017.
Darol and Charlotte stay in close contact, and he considers her a darling and devoted friend.

Darol and Charlotte Pintt Teuscher at The Circle of Hope Benefit Breakfast sponsored by Boys Hope Girls Hope of Kansas City on November 15, 2016 at Indian Hills Country Club.

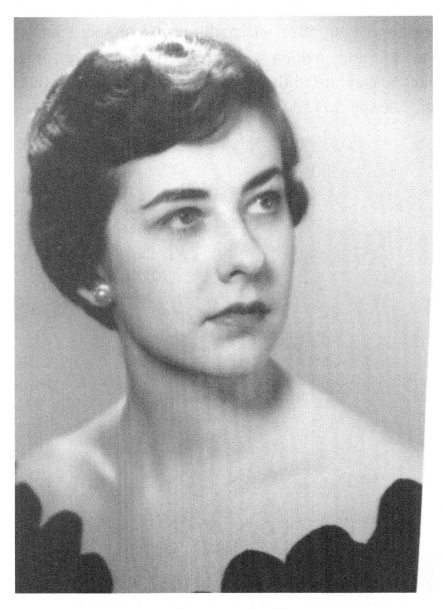

Charlotte Pintt, 1954.

3

ABANDONED IN ARKANSAS

Into hell and out again

When we left the orphanage the second—and last—time, I said goodbye to Miss Pinnt, but I never let go of her message of love and hope. I had no idea just how desperately I would need it in the time to come.

Not long after coming home from the orphanage, Maxine sought to get rid of me again. She saw an ad in the Wichita paper requesting a boy to work on a farm in Arkansas. I was 11 years old when she put me in the car and drove me to Mulvane, Kan., to meet the people who placed the ad. I didn't know what was going on. We didn't talk much on the drive down. All she said was that there were some folks who were going to take care of me in the future.

We pulled up in front of a World War II bungalow type of house. I got out with my little shoebox—just my underwear and socks inside—and walked slowly up to the door. Maxine didn't get out of the car. She'd never even met these people!

I knocked, and a man came to the door, about 6 foot 2 inches, little derby hat and a mustache. "Are you the people who want a boy to go to Arkansas?" I asked.

He said, "Well, yes, come on in. You can call me Uncle Roy, and this here will be Aunt Mary."

I looked up, and my mother was driving away.

I will never, ever forget that moment. I think those feelings will probably linger with me the rest of my life. I was sick inside, just filled with hopelessness. The reality hit me that I could never go home again. It's not that I loved my mother, necessarily, but in that moment I felt completely alone and frightened like never before. It was a shattering sense of being unwanted. I'd just come out of the orphanage, and she'd left me with total strangers. I had no idea what would happen to me. I felt worthless, angry, and desperate. At least when we went to the orphanage, we'd been taken away. But this time Maxine was sending me away—not to stay with family or someone we knew, but with people I'd never met before!

It was clear my mother didn't want me, and that crushed me even more than all the abuse and neglect I'd experienced. Even an abused child still wants his mother to love him. But when a parent has no use for you? To feel total abandonment and the sense that "I don't care if you're alive or dead, Darol. I don't want you around me anymore." That's *devastating.*

I lay in bed that night in Mulvane—don't even remember sleeping. We're going to Arkansas, I thought. Why? I wanted desperately to run away. Felt like a dog trapped in a cage. But I knew if I ran, it might be worse than if I stayed.

The next morning, the three of us headed for a little place off the map called Evening Shade, Ark. I didn't know where in the world that was. I was crammed in the backseat of their two-door car with boxes and things stacked all around me. I made myself as small as possible to fit in that little space. Looking back, I can see what a symbol that was of my childhood. *There's no room for you, Darol*, was the message I'd received over and over again.

It was a long, lonely ride. No one said a word. I was so frightened about what lie ahead. We arrived in

Evening Shade late at night and drove down to a little cabin in a valley. There was one bedroom, a kitchen, and a living room. I slept in a tiny back room—much like a back porch.

The next morning as the sun rose, I discovered a beautiful valley outside my window. That view was a small bright spot during a dark time. In fact, I'd soon discover the beauty of nature would be my only solace in that terrible place.

I didn't get off to a very good start with Aunt Mary and Uncle Roy. They gave me the job of cleaning out the little woodstove in the house, and I didn't really know what I was doing. On one of our first mornings there, I got the bucket and shovel to scoop the coals out, but when I dumped them outside there were some burning embers left over—I didn't know to check for that! Later that day, I was walking home from the school bus and saw smoke down in the valley. I ran toward the house and found the two of them there with a neighbor, desperately fighting the fire with gunnysacks. It came within three or four feet of the house, and it burned in the forest for two weeks. I was beat like a cur dog for that and told over and over how ignorant and stupid I was.

Not long after that, I accidentally left the water spigot on near the chicken coop. We had about 200 baby chicks at the time, and when the water flooded out, it spooked them, and they trampled each other to death. I think Aunt Mary beat me for every one of those dead chickens.

One day Uncle Roy put me on a John Deere tractor and told me to drive. It was a hand clutch, and again, I was clueless. I drove that tractor right through their fence! Somehow, I still have a photo of myself on that John Deere. It's hard to believe Aunt Mary would bother saving something like that, and even harder to imagine how it finally ended up in my hands.

I tried so hard to do things right, but I was still a young boy living in an unfamiliar place with responsibilities I'd never had before. I was bound to forget things and make mistakes, but these weren't the kind of people who had any grace for a child who was still learning.

About a month after we arrived, Uncle Roy left to go back to Wichita for his job. He never came back. I remember Aunt Mary drinking a lot then. I was left alone with a ticking time bomb.

And then summer came—a season of hard labor and little rest. We had two acres of cucumbers that Aunt Mary sold for extra income, and I was responsible for taking care of them. That was a lot of work for an 11-year-old boy—hoeing, picking, and hauling those cucumbers, working in the big patches in the hot sun day after day. Each day I'd go down and pick several big, heavy gunnysacks full of cucumbers. I would push them up on a wooden-wheeled wheelbarrow, load them in the pickup, and we'd go to town to sell them.

Once in town, we'd dump the cucumbers out on a conveyor belt where they'd shimmy back and forth until the smaller ones fell through the holes to be made into pickles. Aunt Mary could get the most money out of those pickle-sized cucumbers. Sometimes, if I hadn't picked the cucumbers at the right time, they'd get too big, and roll right off the conveyor belt. If there were too many big ones, and Aunt Mary didn't make enough money, she'd beat me with a belt when we got home. I remember I couldn't hide those big cucumbers, because she used to watch me pick them. If I tossed them to the side, she'd get after me. If I tried to throw them out, she'd beat me. And if they rolled off the conveyor belt, there'd be hell to pay. It was traumatic, because I knew there'd always be some in the bunch that were too big. They just grew too fast. There was nothing I could do but take a beating.

It was a long, miserable summer.

Soon, an unbearable situation got worse. Aunt Mary began molesting me at night. She'd come into my bedroom on the back porch with an axe, swing it down by my head, and I was so frightened I didn't move. I guess I thought I had no choice. I was trapped—no dad, no mom, nobody to tell. She'd say to me, "If you tell anybody at school, I'll kill you." So I'd go to school and pretend like everything was okay.

I can't emphasize enough the distress of a child who is trapped like that. It's the most overwhelming sense of anxiety to know the abuse is going to happen again and again—be it physical, verbal, sexual, or anything else. I think it's something that never fully leaves a person.

It amazes me that even after the trauma I experienced, I can still recall some things from that time so vividly—brief glimmers of childhood memory that somehow come through. An example of that is the circus we put on in the school gymnasium once. I was the master of ceremonies—had a little black top hat, cane, and coat. I remember the lines exactly:

"Ladies and Gentleman,
we are glad to have you here.
That our circus will please you,
we have no fear..."

I also remember having banty chickens at the farm, about 30 of them, and a little dog named BoBo. A black cat named Smokey slept with me and provided some comfort, even saving my life once. I slept with a heating pad, because I had terrible toothaches and earaches almost every night. One night, Smokey startled me, and just as I sat up, the heating pad burst into flame. Scared me to death.

Not all of the animals I encountered on the farm were friendly, though. We had a mad fox scare, and I was terrified of being bitten. At 6:30 a.m. every weekday morning after school started in the fall, I had to walk alone a mile and a half up out of the valley to catch the school bus. That was a long way in the dark and cold. It felt like an eternity wondering if one of those crazy animals was going to jump out at me. I had trees marked along the way, just in case I had to run and climb to get away.

One of the rabid foxes came all the way up to our house and had her babies under our deck. One day, she came up to feed her babies and my dog, Bobo, attacked her. They fought violently—just rolled around screaming like cats. It was terrifying. We had to quarantine Bobo for 21 days afterward to see if she had rabies. I couldn't pet her or even get near. I'd have to put on a glove and push her food through a little door in the woodshed. It was a miracle to find that Bobo didn't contract rabies.

And it wasn't the only time we fought with life and death on the farm. I remember picking blackberries with Aunt Mary once. We got into a nest of wasps, and she went into anaphylactic shock and passed out. At the time, I didn't know what that was. I thought she had died! I literally picked her up on my shoulder and carried her all the way up the hill to the house. Although she wasn't a big woman, she was much larger than my 11-year-old frame. I laid her on the sofa and put cold, wet rags on her forehead. We had no phone, so I ran to the neighbors' house, about 2 miles away, and they got a doctor. When it was all over, she beat me, because she thought I'd caused it all. But I'm sure I saved her life.

I knew I had to get out of there. I was lonely. I was traumatized by Aunt Mary's abuse and molestation. I'd go to bed at night, knowing she was going to come into my room. I was 12 by then, and all by myself in the world. I was a big kid, who grew fast. Aunt Mary would not buy me clothes or shoes. My mother never sent her money for things like that, and she made a fuss about having to pay for anything for me.

However, my mother would send me a letter occasionally, and though Aunt Mary always crossed out everything that seemed to be good news, I could still see the postmark: Coffeyville, Kan. Never had heard of it, of course, but I knew I had to get away from that hellhole in Arkansas, even if it meant going back to a mother who didn't want me.

There was a bus station in Evening Shade, not far

from the school. One day I mustered up the courage to sneak over there and ask about a ticket. There was a man behind the counter just like you'd see from the movies, complete with a little visor and glasses. I asked him how much it would cost for a one-way trip to Coffeyville. "Two dollars and 79 cents," was his answer.

I had no idea how I'd get the money to buy the bus ticket then, but I soon had it figured out. Every day before and after school, at recess, and lunchtime, we kids shot marbles. We'd carry them in cloth bags on our belts. I wasn't much of a marble shooter, but showing an early entrepreneurial spirit, I figured out how to trade with other people to make a profit.

For every 10 marbles, I could get what was called a cat's eye, and I could sell it to someone for 2 cents. A cat's eye is a special marble—big and pretty with colored glass in the middle. For months, I put my money into a little coffee can under the bed until I'd finally saved enough for a ticket.

I was terrified Aunt Mary would find the coffee can. I was convinced she knew I was trying to run away. If she caught me, I truly believe she would've killed me. And who would've ever known?

When the day came for my escape, I rode to school as usual. It's all a blur to me now, but somehow I got out of the school and made it to the bus station. I remember it was a hot, steamy day and I was trembling...just scared to death. I walked up to the window: "I want to buy a ticket to Coffeyville, Kan.," I said and pushed my $2.79 through to the man.

He said, "Are you traveling alone, little boy?"

I answered, "I'm going to meet my mother."

I got my ticket and slipped around the corner of the building to hide just in case Aunt Mary came to town. I thought for sure she knew, for sure she was coming to get me.

But finally, the bus arrived.

The roads in Evening Shade were dusty dirt roads. I'll never forget the bus coming over the hill that day with a cloud of dust. If you've ever felt like you were getting outta hell, I got outta hell that day. I didn't know what was going to happen to me, but I knew I was getting out of hell.

I often wonder what Aunt Mary must've thought that day. What did she do when I didn't show up after school? Was she surprised? Confused? Grateful? I guess I'll never know.

Many years later I returned to Evening Shade and was flooded with memories in this place where so much had happened to the 11-year-old child I once was.

The little school was still there, and as I walked into the gym, I asked a teacher there what had changed: "This isn't the gym that was here 40 years ago, is it?"

"It's the very same one," he answered.

"But that gym was *enormous*!" As soon as I said it, I realized what had happened. It *was* enormous to the little boy who once stood there. But to the man I had become, it seemed so small.

Not long after that visit, I found a stack of grade cards from my time in Evening Shade. Another moment that flooded me with memories. How in the world, with all my wandering, did those grade cards end up in my possession 60 years later?

Sometimes my experience in Arkansas feels like a nightmare, but when I touch something tangible from that time, I am hit again with the realization that it was all so real. Somehow, against the odds, that little boy survived what was truly a living nightmare.

As I caught the bus out of Evening Shade, I realized I hadn't packed any food, didn't have any money, not a stitch of clothing other than what I was wearing. The driver woke me up in Coffeyville, and I got off wondering what in the world to do next. It never dawned on me that I had no idea where my mother lived in that town. I stole food from a dumpster and slept in a boxcar at the railroad yard.

I looked for my mom for three days. I didn't know she was now living with a man who had the last name of "Vargas." All I knew was to ask for Maxine Rodrock. She had always been a barmaid or a waitress, so I went all around to restaurants and bars asking for her. I stole food wherever I could and slept every night at the railroad yard.

The days blurred together, but after about the third day, someone said, "Sure, I know a Maxine, but she's living with a guy named 'Vargas.'"

So I tracked down the address and knocked on the door. There she stood at the ironing board, staring at me. That image of her is burned into my memory. My mother always ironed in her bra with no blouse on. I don't know why...maybe because we had no air conditioning in those days.

"Mom, I'm home!" I cried.

And she said to me, "What in the f--- are you doing here?"

I was devastated. Literally knocked to the ground.

Why had I run away? She wanted to know. What was wrong with me? Why was I home? We fought all that night, and I knew I couldn't stay.

"Get out, you dirty son-of-a-b----, and don't you ever come back to me!" she yelled.

I felt totally helpless in that moment—completely unwanted. Nowhere to go, no home, no one to help me. All I knew is I'd finally gotten out of Arkansas, and now I had to get the heck out of there.

*Darol and his dog, Bobo, running the tractor
in Evening Shade, Ark., 1955.*

Darol and "Uncle Roy," 1955 in Evening Shade, Ark.

4

RUNAWAY TRAINS

Tracks to nowhere

Next morning, I got up knowing I had to leave. I had no plans of ever coming back—no idea what to do, nowhere to go, no one to call. But I knew I would have no home with my mother ever again. I was 12 years old.

I awoke early and headed down to the railroad yards, before Maxine even got up. Climbed up an empty boxcar, swung over, and landed inside. I didn't know which way it was going. Didn't care. I had absolutely no destination—I was totally aimless and lost. I covered myself with some old empty grain sacks in a corner and hid, waiting to feel that familiar jerk of the train slowly taking off.

Looking back on those moments, I don't know if I was angry or full of fear. I had dreamed of getting out of Arkansas and returning to my family. I was expecting to feel a sense of relief when I walked in, but instead was met with total rejection. I'd been gone for almost a year, every minute of that time desperate to get away from the woman I called Aunt Mary. I guess I never thought of what to expect when I got home. I do know I hated Maxine in that moment, and I was headed anywhere but back to her door.

It's funny. I can't remember even seeing my brother and sisters the night I'd returned, and I had been so lonely for them all that time. I'm not sure they were even there, that's how overwhelming my memories are of Maxine's rejection.

Just 48 hours before I was filled with hope, as I sat on that bus leaving the hell of Arkansas behind me. Now I was scared to death, running away, trapped again. But I knew one thing: I wasn't being hurt in that moment. Nobody was beating me, sexually abusing me, screaming at me. I can't say exactly what I was thinking, but I know my spirit was saying, *"I'm gonna survive. Somehow, I'm gonna make it."*

Days turned into nights. I had no idea where I was or what day it was or where I was going. I was so scared and hungry. I spent days digging through trashcans for scraps of food and huddling in boxcars with my head covered for fear of being discovered.

Sometimes, I rode along with hobos and ate with them at their little campfires in the timber. They'd send me to steal food for them, likely because they knew a little boy had a better chance of getting away with it. It was a strange feeling. Even when there were several of us riding together, we were really all alone. There was never a sense of camaraderie. Hobos usually travel by themselves, and even if they met for a moment on a train, they were always going different ways, just passing through. They were loners, too— cast-offs, alcoholics, unemployed.

I remember most of them being very amiable people. They had their own reasons for hiding, and I don't really remember what they were. Don't even remember anyone talking much. Thankfully, none of them harmed me. I was a big kid for my age—at 12, I looked 15 or 16. I imagine that's why no one messed with me. They probably thought I could defend myself.

It's strange to me that I felt more peaceful on that train, alone with hobos, than I did in Arkansas. But there was a new emptiness—a sense of fear and loneliness I'd never experienced. To this day, the old lonely whistle of a train at night saddens me like nothing else. Even when I'm sitting in my car at the tracks waiting for a train to pass, I'm sometimes filled with that old feeling of isolation and desperation.

It's really hard to explain this feeling to people who've never felt truly alone. I can feel lonely in a room full of people sometimes. I believe there's no more devastating feeling in the world than knowing no one really wants you—that no one cares if you're alive. That kind of pain penetrates the soul.

One day, after weeks of wandering aimlessly, the police picked me up. I think I was on my way back from stealing food when they stopped me. I have no idea where it was—somewhere down south. (Looking back, I'm amazed at how long I travelled on those trains without getting caught. I don't recall seeing a single railroad inspector...no real security to speak of.) I felt so bad about being picked up. The hobos were waiting for me, and I never did get their food back to them.

When the police caught me, I remember being isolated for a day or two, wondering what would happen to me. They threatened saying, "We're going to put you in detention if you don't tell us your name." I refused! It was the first time I really remember standing up for myself. I absolutely did not want to return to Maxine's for fear she would send me back to Arkansas. And I was determined to stay out of reform school, because I feared ending up like my dad, who'd

I CAN AND I WILL

been in prison. Once again, I was trapped. I had nowhere to go.

Finally, I had to tell them who I was, and they took me to Iola, Kan., to where Maxine had moved. Somehow in the time I'd been gone, she had moved from Coffeyville back to Iola. She told me I'd been gone for weeks, and she was furious. I honestly think she was angry I was still alive, that she just couldn't get rid of me.

Looking back, my 11th and 12th years were probably the loneliest and most traumatic of my entire life. Even early childhood in the orphanage didn't create that sense of loneliness I had in Arkansas and riding all those trains. I missed Beverly, Donnie, and Barbara so badly. I guess I just finally realized there was no home, no family for me.

Sometimes I think that whole experience of running away made me tough—maybe too tough. I feel like I could handle anything you throw at me today. But other times I feel like it made me weak. I really don't know to this day which one it is. I'm sure a lot of children and adults who've survived abuse, neglect, abandonment, and rejection vacillate between those feelings—being too strong and too weak. We have strength enough to have survived the trauma, but we're also dealing with the pain and vulnerability that comes from living through it. This leaves us feeling completely unsure of ourselves.

There are days when I feel worthless, overwhelmed, frightened, rejected—and so vulnerable. I just want to go find a corner and hide. Few people see that in me, though, which has made me realize that lots of people are probably carrying things others can't see. Some have experienced worse trauma than what I've been through, others less. But the fact is, the scars are always there.

Darol at age 12

OUT OF THE SHADOW

5

OPEN DOORS, OPEN HEARTS

The people who changed my life along the way

My story is a powerful illustration of what can happen when we open our hearts to someone in need. After surviving those early years of abuse, loneliness, neglect, and abandonment, I was blessed to encounter some patient, loving souls. Each has, in his or her own way, helped me take one more step out of my dark past and toward a brighter future.

I had just been returned after running away on the trains, but I knew I couldn't live with Maxine. I was fortunate that my Great Aunt Pearline and Uncle Raymond Stephens (my mother's uncle) reached out. When I was younger, I had gone to stay at their farm outside Garnett, Kan., for a few weeks in the summer, and, once again, they welcomed me into their family.

Uncle Raymond was a hard-working farmer, and Aunt Pearline was a darling lady—at 5 feet tall she was the strongest little woman I've ever known. They had six kids—five girls and a boy. It was tight quarters, with two adults and seven kids and no indoor plumbing, all sharing an outhouse. There was no running water, just an outside pump from a well. Except for my time in the orphanage, I'd never had indoor plumbing or running water.

But my cousins were so welcoming and always accepted me. I dearly loved living with them. It was there that I developed a love for agriculture, cattle, and horses. I learned to milk cows and pick corn. We milked 56 cows every morning and night, by hand. I definitely learned the value of hard work!

We kept chickens, and every so often Aunt Pearline would chop the head off one to eat. They would flop around for five minutes, so I learned what it meant to "run around like a chicken with its head cut off." Also, Aunt Pearline would cut off the roosters' combs and lower legs. She'd boil them in some kind of seasoning, and after school, we kids would suck and chew on them. Quite tasty, as I remember.

54

The family had three horses: Trigger, Queenie, and Midnight. My only male cousin, Eugene, and I used to ride them without saddles or bridles. We'd take bailing twine off a bale of hay, wrap it around the horses' noses, make reins, and ride around like Native Americans. We'd run wild up and down the hills, jump through the creeks, and race each other through the woods. We had to ride to the top of a high hill to bring the cows back down through the timber. The thick tree branches would knock us off, but we always got back up.

(Those times on horseback would end up serving me well. I became a very good horseman, and eventually won the Quarter Horse Congress, the largest Western pleasure horse show in the world, and the Super Stakes, one of the largest cutting shows in the world. It's fun to think it all started in those childhood days riding bareback.)

I didn't know a thing about showing horses back on the farm, but I showed Queenie once at the Kincaid Kansas County Fair. She was a one-eyed horse that Uncle Raymond spoiled—by feeding her carrots and apples all the time. Queenie knew if she saw Raymond, she'd surely be getting what she wanted. So here I am trying to show my very first horse at the fair, and Uncle Raymond shows up with his carrots and apples. Every time we'd come around the pen, Queenie would slow down and sidle up beside Uncle

Raymond. Everybody'd laugh as I'd kick her and say, "C'mon, horse!" Then off we'd go for another round.

In the fall, we kids walked two miles home each day from our one-room schoolhouse called Minkler Star. There were eight students enrolled in the school; three of them were my cousins. (I'm one of the very few people in my generation who was born at home and went to a one-room schoolhouse!) Mrs. Lavon Robinson was my teacher there, and while I didn't know it yet, she would come to have a very big impact in my life.

Even though the Stephens family was good to me, I ran off. By that time, I imagine I'd developed a mindset that I'd eventually be rejected anywhere I went. Maybe it was my way of trying to protect myself from more hurt.

It wasn't until 50 years later, near the end of Aunt Pearline's life, that she asked me why I ran away. She was lying in her hospital bed, just a few nights before she died. She rolled over and told me she was ready to go, that she'd given up and was tired of fighting. She took my hand, and in her squeaky little voice said, "Darol, honey, why'd you run off and leave us all those years ago? I loved you so much."

I didn't really know how to answer. I looked her in the eyes and told her I guess I just ran away from everything. I'd loved her all my life and was always so thankful for what she'd done for me. Tears welled up

I CAN AND I WILL

in her eyes, and I don't think it was until that moment that I learned how much she truly loved me. She was such a kind soul, so soft and tender. It warmed my heart to see the love in her eyes.

It was Halloween night in 1956 when I ran away from Aunt Pearline and Uncle Raymond's. I was 12 years old. My sister, Beverly, and her husband, Max, had been visiting Iola (where Maxine lived at the time), and I got it in my head to run off and stay with Beverly. There was no good reason for leaving my aunt, uncle, and cousins. Everything had been fine.

But Beverly and Max took me home to live with them in Seneca, Mo. They were married when Beverly was just 14. Max was a good man to take me in. Here he'd just married my sister, and her little brother shows up to live with them.

Although Max was young, he did his best to take me under his wing and teach me a few things. Down in the part of Missouri where they lived it's solid timber, and back then there were squirrels everywhere. He'd take me squirrel hunting, giving me a single shot .22 rifle and one bullet.

"You're gonna learn to use a rifle," he told me. "You get one shot. If you don't get a squirrel, you might not eat supper tonight, Darol," he'd laugh. The lesson, of course, was that sometimes you only get one chance to do things right. Max only had a 10th-grade education, but he was one of the smartest men I ever met.

There were Native American mound graves all over the land we hunted. I remember we'd sit on those mounds and talk. Looking back, I realize how good (and rare!) it was for me to have that kind of connection with a young man like him. He was almost like a father figure, as he was nearly 22 and I was 12. Most days I missed a lot of squirrels, but I always seemed to find a way to get supper anyhow!

I'll never forget the first day of school that year. We were so close to the Oklahoma-Missouri line that even though we lived in Seneca, Mo., I'd take a 12-mile bus ride to Wyandotte, Okla., for school. I walked in for the first time on a Monday, and the minute I arrived a bell went off. Everyone got up and walked out. I looked around nervously and asked the teacher, "What happened? What happened? Are we having a fire drill?"

She said, "We're having a school walk-out, because we won the state championship in football last Friday night."

So I walked out. But there was no bus to take, no parent to greet me, no friend to follow. I had no idea where I was or how to get back to Max and Beverly's. I asked someone where Seneca was, and he pointed in a general direction, "Over there somewhere." I was used to running off, being on my own and just trying to find my way. So I just started walking. Had to figure out a way to make it home and somehow got to Beverly's by 10 p.m. that night. She was scared to death. I was so mad about what had happened, I didn't ever want to go back to that school.

When I did finally return a week or two later, I saw a football for the first time in my life. I was a big 7th grader, and one day the football coach just threw me the ball and said, "See if you can make it to the goal line." It was a tackling drill, and when the other boys tried to tackle me, I literally ran over them on my way to the goal.

I said, "Give me that football back," and took off again down the field.

That was a little highlight of my short time there—being introduced to a sport I would later love playing and coaching. Excelling at something always lifted me up. I was faster than anybody else in that class, and I could run a football. When you don't feel like you have much else going for you, every little bit makes a difference.

Still, I ended up dropping out of school and staying home with Beverly. I wasn't always the easiest kid to have around. Tried not to look for trouble, but somehow it found me.

Max's extended family had walnut trees on their property, and at some point each boy in the family would claim his own tree. Once a tree was claimed, everyone knew whose it was, and there was an unwritten rule that you didn't mess with anybody else's tree. When these trees produced walnuts, you could collect and sell them for $2 a sack. That was big money for us! If you sold the walnuts already hulled, you'd get $4 a sack—even bigger money!

(Have you ever tried to crack and hull a gunnysack full of walnuts? I'll tell you, it isn't easy. We had a little trick to speed up the process. We'd raise a car up on blocks and start the tires spinning and feed the walnuts through the tires. The spinning would loosen the hulls up and spit them out. Don't know how someone figured that trick out, but it sure worked like a charm.)

Since I wasn't from that area, I didn't have a tree of my own. But, being the determined, sly kid I was, I'd wait 'til everyone was sleeping, grab a flashlight, and go out to pick up walnuts from other people's trees. Max's nephews each had a tree, and I helped myself to theirs frequently. When Max figured out what I was doing, he warned me, "Darol, those trees belong to those boys. Forever. They were born and raised here, and they have claimed them."

I said, "I know, Max." And then I went right back to picking up the walnuts, and those boys would come over and just beat the tar out of me. So finally, I made a plan, and the next time those walnuts matured and fell, I went out again after dark. But I knew those boys would be coming for me. So I had a baseball bat ready for them. I was ready to defend myself—and I did. They didn't bother me anymore after that.

That's how I fought when I was a kid—quick and mean. When you fight enough, you become a scrapper. You learn that if you don't hit the hardest, you'll end up on the ground first.

Needless to say, the walnut incident caused a little bit of trouble. And that wasn't the only kind of trouble I created for Beverly and Max. I was belligerent and insolent toward my sister. Even though I was living with her, she was still my big sister. I think it was simply too much for a young couple to deal with, especially with Beverly being just 15 and Max 22.

Beverly finally had to ask me to leave. We all were in agreement that the situation simply wasn't working. It was so hard for me to go, because she had always been that constant, caring, motherly presence for me. I was devastated. But looking back, I see that it was something that needed to happen. Maxine came around to get me, and once more I felt adrift.

Beverly and Max stayed in the Ozark area all of their lives, where Max worked in construction, operating heavy machinery. They raised a family of three children and many grandchildren. I always felt welcome to come back and visit with Beverly and Max. And Beverly and I are close to this day.

Beverly, Max, and their son Jimmy Dale in 1956.

Aunt Pearline and Uncle Raymond Stephens in the 1970's.

Darol and his Aunt Pearline.

OUT OF THE SHADOW

6

LAVON AND RAY

A family to call my own

After leaving Max and Beverly's, I was more or less homeless again. I couldn't go back to Aunt Pearline and Uncle Raymond's, because I'd embarrassed myself by running off when I knew I shouldn't have. Had no idea where I was going, what I was going to do in my life, but I knew damn good and well I wasn't going to stay with Maxine. I was like a worthless stranger to her.

Lavon Robinson (my schoolteacher when I'd lived on the farm with the Stephens) had gone to Maxine and said, "If you can find Darol, we'll see if we can help him." And sure enough, when I made my way home, Lavon and her husband, Ray, took me in to live with them on their farm outside Garnett, Kan.

They'd never had children, so when I came into their lives, it was a blessing for them. And I was blessed to have them, too. Lavon had two brothers and one sister, and they all loved and accepted me as one of their own. And though I didn't realize it back then, their love would literally change my life.

Lavon was the sister who always had everyone to her house. She hosted all the get-togethers and big dinners. Every weekend the whole family was there. In fact, when I moved in, she had a big gathering so everyone—aunts, uncles, and cousins—could greet me. They all clapped excitedly when I walked in the door. They were truly happy to welcome me into the family. Lavon put her arm around me to introduce me to everyone, but I was overwhelmed. I remember thinking, "I've gotta get out of here..." I walked right through the house and out the back door. Lavon's niece, Judy, followed me, took my hand, and sat beside me on a propane tank. Everyone was worried I'd run off again. I'd been such a loner for so long.

I came to live with Lavon and Ray on Dec. 12, 1956. I believe that if I hadn't, I'd have easily ended up in reform school. There was just no place to go. Lavon and Ray were exactly who I needed in my life.

In fact, when I was 14, they took me to a lawyer,

who turned to me and said, "Lavon and Ray have talked with your mom. They want to adopt you and give you their last name: Robinson."

I have no idea why I said: "I don't want to be adopted. Someday I'm going to be proud of the Rodrock name." Perhaps my 14-year-old self had a sense of the future.

As many a teacher, Lavon was incredibly patient. I was way behind in school. I'd been sent to 11 schools—*some twice*—before the 8th grade and hadn't attended the last one much because of running away. She helped me make up for a lot of what I'd missed, working with me at home for hours with flashcards. Lavon always helped me believe I was smart and that I could learn, regardless of my past."

There were only eight kids in our little one-room school. We'd all sit at our desks until our grade was called, and then we'd go to the table in front for our lesson. There were two students in my grade level— Rosalie, my second cousin, and me. One day, during our class time, we were talking about the Civil War and the abolitionist John Brown. "Darol," Lavon called on me, "would you please explain to us who John Brown was?"

I had no clue. "Well," I answered, "I'm guessin' if his name was John he must've been a man..."

She slammed that book shut so fast, "*You take*

your seat, Darol Rodrock!"

Lavon was as kind as they come, but she sure had a way of keeping me in line. She was stern when she had to be. She had high expectations and was proud of her profession. She was a 2-year certified teacher. In the Depression, they were so short of teachers that if you got two years of college, they'd give you a degree automatically. Lavon was underpaid all of her life because of that, but she didn't let it stop her from being a caring and dedicated teacher. She taught for 41 years in Kansas elementary schools.

Ray, meanwhile, had a 10th grade education. He'd farmed all his life. He was struggling financially at the time I moved in, but of course I didn't know it. He had a Grade "A" dairy farm. As far as I was concerned, he seemed a rich man.

Ray was a happy guy who enjoyed life. As hard as he worked every day, he still found time for fun. One day I was out milking one of our cows in the barn. Ray walked in, so I decided to be ornery and squirt him in the face with the milk. The next day, when it was Ray's turn to milk, I walked in and he threw the whole *bucketful* of milk in my face! That was Ray—always making someone laugh.

I have so many stories about him, but this one is my favorite. I don't even remember exactly how it happened, but it's a perfect illustration of how he made me feel: One day we were driving along in his old pickup and Ray was humming. He hummed and whistled all the time, and it irritated me when I was in one of my teenage moods. I grumbled, "What're you so happy about, Ray?"

He put his hand over on my shoulder and said, "I'm happy just because you're in my life, Darol." Can you imagine how I felt? *He was happy simply because I was there.*

That's the feeling he always gave me. I didn't have to do anything except just be there with him. Didn't have to make my bed or get straight A's or be the best at anything. Just be myself, and that was enough.

Even with all the loving care the two of them showed me, I still ran away from time to time—just headed off down the road. That was the way I'd lived for so long. Lavon and Ray never knew what I'd been through, and I never talked about Arkansas or the trains. They just knew I was struggling and could be very emotional at times. I'd run off and Ray would come look for me. He'd pull up beside me as I walked along the road, roll down the window and say, "Havin' a hard time, aren't you, bud? Wanna come home?"

I'd never had someone come after me. Nobody ever cared if I was gone. It brings tears to my eyes today, because I think of how he could've reacted. "You dumb kid, get back here...where ya goin'?" That's the kind of response I'd been used to all my life.

There's a funny saying Ray used to use when I'd try to run away: We had a lot of cats on the farm, and there was one tomcat that kept killing kittens. I kind of hate to tell this story these days, but one day Ray tied that cat in a gunny sack, put it in the back of the Chevrolet, drove it 16 miles to town, and dumped the cat. Didn't even open the gunnysack when we got there!

Six weeks later, that cat walked right back into our yard. Ray would tease me, "You're just like that damn tomcat. Just keep comin' back don't you?" He'd laugh and chuckle and love me. "You just always find your way home somehow, don't you Darol? And you're always welcome, and we're always here for you."

The Robinsons loved me unconditionally. They gave me a place that felt like home and always took me back in. Maybe they could see the insecurity that I carried inside. It wasn't about them. It was about me learning to trust and finally believing I could belong somewhere.

So I started to find my place there at Minkler Star, that little one-room rural school in the Kincaid, Kan., district. And I turned out to be a pretty good athlete. Back then Anderson County had a track meet each year. Most counties at that time had lots of small schools, and every spring they'd all come together for a meet. Ray helped me train for that track meet in his own innovative way. To make a shot put, he took the handle off his sledgehammer and had me throw the head part. A regular shot put was 8 pounds; that sledgehammer head was 12. After getting used to that heavier weight, an 8-pound shot put felt like a piece of nothing in my hands. So I set a record in the shot put.

He trained me for running events in old knee-high farm boots. Made me run in them every night. He'd say, "When you take those old boots off and put shoes on, they'll feel light as a feather!" I'd run down our lane that was about a half mile from the road—run all the way down and back in those big, heavy rubber boots. Sure enough, when it came time to wear track shoes, I felt like I didn't have a thing on.

Ray didn't know anything about track, but he figured it all out for me. He was something else. Didn't matter that he never made it through school. He was resourceful, and he taught himself a lot in life. I'm so grateful that he took the time to teach me, too.

That spring of 1958, I won four purple ribbons at the meet, set a record, and of all things, broke my arm! The high jump record was 5 feet 2 inches, and I was determined to break it at that meet. Sure enough, I cleared it, and someone said, "You oughtta see if you can jump higher and set a new record!"

So I cleared 5 foot 4 inches and kept going. When I went on to 5 foot 6 inches, I missed it the first time. Came around again and cleared it on my second try.

Back then, we didn't do the "Fosbury Flop" like they do now. We did the scissors. When you landed, you landed on your butt. And when I cleared that last height, 5 foot 6 inches, I landed with my left arm down and felt something crack.

I remember standing up, hearing everybody's cheers. All of a sudden I felt woozy, and then I passed out cold. They all thought I was so happy I fainted! They taped my four purple ribbons to my cast that day, snapped a photo, and captured a memory.

GARNETT HIGH SCHOOL

Ray Meyer, the football coach from Garnett, was at that Anderson County track meet and saw me compete. He encouraged me to come to Garnett, and he talked Lavon and Ray into sending me to school there. (We joked that I was the first recruit in Garnett high-school history, since I was coming from a different school district!) The Robinsons would drive me the 15 miles to Garnett each morning, and the football coach would drive me all the way home after track.

But during my sophomore year, everything changed. I came home one cold Friday night in

January after a basketball game and discovered all we owned on the farm lined up outside. We were having a dispersal sale. We were bankrupt, and Ray had lost the farm. They hadn't said a word about it. I was in total shock.

Out of the blue, we packed up and left. I'll never forget how upsetting that move was for me. I finally felt settled after years of being passed around and running away. Here I was a sophomore, starting in football, lead in the musical, I'd lettered in track, sang in the choir. I finally felt like I'd found my place. It was hard to leave the farm. I had to say goodbye to my favorite animal there, a Guernsey heifer I'd raised myself. I had to say goodbye to the friends I'd finally started feeling attached to. Everything I'd begun to hold onto was taken away. I felt lost, lonely, and discouraged.

Darol's class picture with Lavon Robinson, his teacher and foster mom. Three of the girls in the class were his cousins: Rosalee, Joann, and Ruby Stephens (daughters of Pearline and Uncle Raymond) circa 1958.

Darol and his prized heifer, Debbie, 1958 Grand Champion, at the Anderson County Fair.

Darol and Ray in Jan. 1958.

Darol and Lavon, Darol's foster mom.

Lavon and Roy, Darol's foster parents for life,
as pictured in 1980.

Darol's one room schoolhouse, Minkler Star,
in Anderson County, 1957-58.

7

MARYSVILLE, KANSAS
A little town with a big heart

The next day, we packed up and moved to Marysville, Kan., a tiny town right on 36 Highway, north of Manhattan. It seemed to be out in the middle of nowhere. It was a cold, dreary winter night when we pulled into town: Jan. 20, 1960, right in the middle of a blizzard—there was 20 inches of snow on the ground that year. Lavon and Ray had enough money left to buy or lease a Dairy Queen, and we moved into a little white house right behind it. I felt disconnected, lonely, and frightened.

One of the first weekends after moving in, I went to a youth event at the Lutheran church. I walked in to this kids' gathering in my boots and jeans, with no clue what to expect. Didn't know a soul. A pretty blue-eyed girl walked up to me and said, "You must be new here."

And I said, "Yes, I am. My name's Darol Rodrock."

And she said "Well I'm Lois, and I'm gonna be your friend for the rest of your life. Come and make yourself at home."

And she was right. Lois and her husband, Duane, are still my friends 55 years later. Lois represented the spirit of kindness and hospitality that I found in Marysville. At that time in my life, I was so insecure. I'd run away from everywhere, wasn't stable or sure of myself at all, never thought I'd find a place to truly call "home." But like Lois, the people of Marysville reached out their hands in welcome and said, "C'mon Darol, you'll be our friend for life." Even though no one there knew what I'd been through, they truly made me feel like I was one of them.

We arrived in January, and by April 1st my classmates had elected me junior class president for the following year. I didn't have any idea what that was. Lavon and Ray were not very sophisticated and with my background, neither was I. I'd see pictures around the high-school walls with my name, "Rodrock," on them and wonder what it was all about. So there I was, elected class president, with no idea what to do. Junior Prom rolled around and the girls let me know I was in charge of that event. I remember thinking, "Prom? What in the world is a prom?" The next year I was elected vice president of the student council.

No one in Marysville knew where I'd come from— what I'd been through. They knew I had foster parents, but that was it. I was seen as a friendly, confident guy, but I was carrying a lot of pain that I masked. I felt like a total outsider. Walked through the halls in my boots and jeans, toothpick in my mouth— that's how people dressed where I'd come from. But Marysville was a classy town. They wore khakis and loafers.

Despite the fact I felt like I didn't fit in, I learned and loved so many things during my short time there. I loved playing football at the stadium. It was the last year of renowned coach Homer Hanson's teaching career, and I had the privilege of getting to know him before he retired. Coach Hanson won 48 straight football games at MHS—he never lost a game. He was a great individual and had a lasting impact on generations. He talked real slow and always had these fun sayings. *"You never can tell the depth of the well by the length of the handle on the pump."* And *"You know, if you want the best apple on the tree, sometimes you've got to climb a little higher."* Because the best apple is right at the top, he told us. If we weren't willing to climb to the top, we may never get the best or be the best.

Coach Hanson's only son, who was also named Darrel, was killed in an accident not long before we moved to town. And here I was, a Darol who came into his life two years later. He took a liking to me. I was like his Darrel, a hard worker and a student leader. I think it was a healing relationship for both of us.

I got into track again, won second in State in the half mile and was part of the state championship relay team. (By the way, that state record still stands!) I had the chance to connect with a great bunch of hard-working guys on that track team. One of them, Ron Grauer, was one of my biggest encouragers. He was a senior when I was a junior. I beat him every time we ran, but he always lifted me up. He'd tell me how proud he was of me and thank me for challenging him to run harder. He's a great guy and still a friend today. (As a matter of fact, it's his lovely daughter, Paige, who's helping me write this!)

One of my favorite track memories happened at the State indoor meet in Manhattan my sophomore year. Lavon and Ray were there, cheering me on as always. I ran the mile, and when I came around the corner, Lavon was sitting right in the front yelling "GO

DAROL, GO DAROL, GO DAROL!" at the top of her lungs. I was so embarrassed—I could hear her voice all the way around the track. I came back down the straightaway and there she was again—she'd followed me! At the end of my time in high-school track, Lavon gave me a gift I'll always treasure: She collected all the small medals we received at each track meet and made me a bracelet out of them. She wore it to all my meets. It meant so much that she took the time to do that for me. No one in my life had ever shown me how much they cared like Lavon and Ray.

Two other folks who truly helped me to see the best in myself during that time were Dr. and Mrs. Thomas. I dated their daughter, Ginny, and they welcomed me as part of their family. Dr. Thomas was a professional through and through and was kind enough to share a lot of wisdom that still inspires me as a businessman today. I remember he had this funny way of closing his eyes when he talked to you, but he knew what he was saying, and I didn't miss a word.

"You know Darol," he'd say squinting his eyes, "if you're going to be successful, you have to learn to talk to anybody on their level. Don't talk above them, and don't talk below them. You'll talk to all kinds in your life—smart people, and not-so-smart people, rich people, poor people. You just have to meet them where they are." (He was a doctor, and that was what he'd learned to do to connect with his patients.) I never forgot that, and it has had a huge influence on my life, not only in the world of business, but also in my day-to-day relationships with people.

I remember Ginny and I came home to the Thomas' house from a date one weekend. There happened to be a fraternity event at the University of Kansas a few hours away in Lawrence the next night, and Dr. Thomas knew I was interested in joining. He threw me the keys to his brand new 1962 Bonneville and said, "Here, son, you and Ginny have a good time..." Can you imagine what that meant to a kid like me?

Later in life, I learned that Dr. Thomas' parents had died young, and he'd been raised by his aunt and uncle. I often wonder if he saw himself in me. Regardless, the Thomas family was a gift to me. They helped me believe I was somebody, and could be somebody. Even though Ginny and I grew up and went our separate ways, we were blessed to become lifelong friends.

Reverend Brady is another person I will never forget from that time in my life. He was pastor of the Marysville United Methodist Church. He taught me a lot about Jesus and helped me believe I could do anything I wanted in life. He showed me how to be a leader, how to stand up in front of people, and how to speak and inspire them. I actually earned a local preacher's license for a brief time, and I conducted sermons at the Oketo United Methodist Church. I'd often speak at churches around the area, sharing the message: "Be ye not conformed to the world, but live in the spirit of Jesus Christ" [Romans, 12:2]. It's a message I was passionate about—and still am today.

The Future Farmers of America instructor, Mr. Larson, also got me involved in speech and gave me opportunities to talk to the Kiwanis, the Rotary, and other venues where I could develop my speaking skills. I was in both the Ag department and the athletic department, which was very unusual for someone in those days. I think it's one of the reasons I made so many friends. I could talk with the farmers because I knew farming, and I could connect with the athletes, because I knew their world, too. I'm still that way. I love the diversity of my friendships. They all bring out something different in me, and I learn from each of their unique perspectives.

Everyone in Marysville had their own way of making me feel a part of that town, and I have never forgotten one of them. Together, those friends helped me develop a positive self-image for the first time in my life. I could've so easily turned into a rebel, become bitter toward people and angry at the world, but being a part of a loving community kept me from that. I will always be thankful that my foster parents chose Marysville. If they'd chosen another place, I wonder if it would've made such an impact on my life.

Lavon and Ray continued to support, nurture, and love me unconditionally. They believed the very best about me, recognized my potential, lifted me up, and encouraged me no matter what I did. They saw me through high school and beyond. They were my loving parents, and I cared for them both throughout their lives.

One cold January morning in 1980, I woke up and told my wife, "I'm going to Lavon and Ray's today."

She said, "You can't! It's Friday. The kids are in school." (We had always gone to visit as a family.) But I felt strongly about going that day, so I made the hour-and-a-half trip to Iola alone. We had a wonderful time together—laughed and cried, told stories of all we'd shared together through the years. I spent the whole day there, and after thanking them for everything they'd done for me in my life, I headed home with my heart full.

The following Monday, the phone rang. "Darol, you'd better come quick," It was Lavon's brother George. "Ray just had a heart attack, and you may not make it in time." Sure enough, when I arrived, Ray was already gone. But I had such a sense of peace and gratitude. What a gift that just two days earlier we'd been blessed with a beautiful "goodbye." Something in my spirit had said, *Go. Thank Ray for all he's done—for the life and the love he gave you.* It was a powerful reminder for me that we should always share our love and gratitude with each other while we are able—we never know when it will be our last chance.

Years later, another special thing happened after Lavon died. I found a box under her bed full of everything she'd collected for me over the years. Trophies, medals, photos—somehow even my grade cards from that dark time in Arkansas had made it into her hands. (To this day, I don't know how those grade cards made their way from Aunt Mary to Lavon!) It was just by chance I stumbled upon these things. I'd gone through everything and found one last box to go through. I feel it was somehow meant to be.

When I discovered all those treasures from my early life, it helped me to put some pieces back together. I realized again how much Lavon and Ray loved me like their own son. I owe them so much for what they did for me. If I hadn't ended up with them, life would've certainly been different.

*Darol and Reverend Brady and his wife Barbara, 2016.
Reverend Brady was pastor at the Maryville's United Methodist
Church.*

Darol with Dr. and Mrs. Thomas in the 1990's.

Darol, running track in Marysville his Junior Year.

Darol's graduation photo, 1962.

Darol's senior year in Marysville playing football, 1962.

OUT OF THE SHADOW

8

STRUGGLE, SACRIFICE, & SUCCESS

Becoming a college graduate

We left Marysville shortly after graduation—another change I wasn't prepared for. The van came to move us to Iola, and I said goodbye to a town that had truly changed my life. I'd lived there only 30 months, but it sure seemed like a lot longer than that. The friends I made there, the people who influenced me, and the love I received from them all have been with me for a lifetime.

I entered the University of Kansas that fall and was recruited and pledged into the Beta Theta Pi fraternity house. It was the number-one scholarship fraternity at KU at the time. I didn't really feel I belonged at KU, and I sure didn't belong with the Betas. (The Thomas family had helped me through the process, as their son was a Beta.) All the young men there were extremely smart, high achievers. They'd won the Hill Football Intramural Championship and the Scholarship Cup (both prestigious awards on campus) for many years in a row. As a Phys Ed major, I didn't really fit in. I was more country, wearing boots and jeans. Probably should've gone to K-State, though if I'd ended up elsewhere, I doubt I would've ever graduated.

Being around the other guys there, all so smart and determined, made me study harder. They truly inspired me. Every night we studied from 6:30 to 10:30 p.m., no matter what. Sometimes we studied all night.

The whole college experience was extremely difficult for me. During my sophomore year, I met and fell in love with my wife, Karen. We were married during my junior year, and I moved out of the fraternity and into a home in Overland Park, Kan. At one point, I was driving back and forth some 40 miles each way, every day. Put myself through college with a national defense loan and a 40-hour-a-week job at a grocery store. I had a final the day after our first child was born!

I lettered in wrestling and track and travelled with the a cappella choir. I was in ROTC there for two years and was a champion map reader. It's funny, today I could tell you the topography of any piece of ground just by looking at it, which works out well with the business I'm in!

The one thing I didn't have to contend with, blessedly, was the war. I didn't go to Viet Nam, because I became a schoolteacher after graduation. Coupled with my being married and having kids, it kept me at the bottom of the Marshall county draft board. I didn't know that at the time, though, and worried constantly about it.

I graduated in four years, earning 124 college credit hours on the button. Even made the honor roll my last semester. A lot of kids today don't graduate in four years, but I had to—I had no choice.

People often ask me how I balanced it all in college. "Why did you stay?" they ask. "Why didn't you just give up and drop out?" I tell them I didn't balance it all. I just survived.

Heck no, it wasn't easy. I missed my foster parents. Felt like a fish out of water. (Did you know that according to the Jim Casey Youth Opportunities

Initiative, there's less than a 3% chance for foster children to earn a college degree in their lifetime?) But here's what I tell people today: If you're going to make it through the most challenging times, you've got to have a goal that is important and meaningful to you. I kept moving forward 'cause I knew what I wanted. I wanted an education, because I somehow knew it was the only way to leave my past behind me. And I wanted to coach—I had a vision for my life that I wasn't about to give up for anything.

I read a story awhile back about a professional football player: 35 years old, 5 foot 9 inches, 170 pounds. He goes to the swimming pool every day, puts 40-pound weights on, sinks to the bottom where it's 10 feet deep, squats down and tries to push himself to the surface of the water a hundred times. A hundred times a day! Think of the determination that takes. Pure grit. I guess that's what I had, too, looking back on it.

I remember on the last day of fraternity pledge training, I got into a fight with one of the Betas (who actually became my good friend later!). The vote was coming down, and a lot of the guys wanted to kick me out of the fraternity for fighting. One of them stood up and said, "We need Darol. We need guys in this house with a lot of grit." And I'm still proud to be a Beta today.

One of my former fraternity brothers, John, emailed recently, and I was humbled by his words. *"I'm not big on reunions..."* he said, *"but one regret I have is that I have missed shaking your hand and looking you in the eye to tell you how proud I am that we were once pledge brothers at KU...When I left in '65 I was confident that you would make an impact on our world, Darol. So, it's really no surprise to learn what you have done with your life...The Yiddish term for a guy like this is a mensch. Look it up. It means a stand-up guy...a person of honor and integrity. That's how the world should regard you. I know I always have."*

I'd never thought about the impression I'd made on my fraternity brothers—only how thankful I was for what they did for *me*! The whole experience taught me that if I want to improve myself, I needed to challenge myself to seek out people like my fraternity brothers. Being around young men who took the initiative with their education made me want to be a better student than I otherwise might've been. There were 21 guys in my pledge class. A large percentage are doctors, lawyers, and PhD's today—very smart, dedicated men. And while that's just not who I am—the intellectual type—they inspired me to graduate and to not lose sight of my goal. And for that I will always be grateful.

Turkey Pull
December 20, 1962

Darol and Ginny at the annual Beta Theta Phi Christmas Party in 1962.

The Beta Theta Pi House at the University of Kansas in 1962.

Ginny Thomas, her parents Dr. and Mrs. Thomas & her brother, Bob,
who was Darol's pledge father at the Beta Theta Pi House at K.U.

Mike Vineyard, Darol, and Al Simmons as Darol receives the Beta Man of the Year award in 2017.

9

THE RISE OF RODROCK DEVELOPMENT

The evolution from teacher, to homebuilder, to developer

Telling the story of my young life still amazes me. I look at where the journey has brought me—from a childhood that held little hope for a meaningful future to a life many would consider a success—and I know what a blessing it has been.

But as with most things, my road to success started first as a small, winding path. I got my first teaching job in Hillcrest Junior High School in Shawnee Mission, Kan. It was a big job for me, and I was so thrilled to be in the Shawnee Mission School District, because back then they weren't hiring much. I taught physical education, which was called "health" at that time. I got along great with the other teachers. In fact, I'm still friends with some of them. That was 1966!

I then went to Turner High School in Turner, Kan., and got a head coaching job in wrestling and an assistant coaching job in football. It was a different kind of district for me, but we had a lot of success in wrestling, and we were second in the league—almost beating the defending state champions!

Still, I was excited to come back to Shawnee Mission West that next year, because they'd just started a wrestling program. They'd never had wrestling before, but I'd lettered in wrestling in college, so I had some idea of what it was about.

But truthfully, I didn't know near as much as I thought I did. We didn't win any duels at Shawnee Mission West for two years. Our kids had no uniforms, they wrestled in their gym uniforms, with no headgear, and we taped the gym mats together. It was kind of a ridiculous thing, but that's the way we started it out. Eventually, I coached the wrestling team to win numerous state championships. It's safe to say I learned a lot about the sport during my time there.

In addition to wrestling, I was an assistant football coach. For the first two years, I coached for free. I wanted the job, but there were no openings, so I went to Dick Purdy, our football coach at the time (and—later in life—a Hall of Fame coach in Kansas), and told him I'd coach for free if he had any need for me. I'd played football at KU and in high school. I loved coaching and teaching, and I thought I'd do that the rest of my life. I was taking graduate classes at KU, finishing my master's degree in 1973.

Believe it or not, I still have a stub of my first paycheck from my first year of teaching. I took home $360 a month. Didn't seem like very much money when rent was $85, the car payment was $55, plus utilities and food and clothes and one thing and another. During my years as a young teacher, I struggled to make ends meet. It's a great profession to help kids, but you're never making quite enough money to have a comfortable life, especially when you're trying to support a family. In fact, I worked at a grocery store stocking shelves during the summer to make it through.

We couldn't make ends meet the first year I coached at Shawnee Mission West. I was making $4,800, maybe $5,000, and that was gross, before taxes. So there sure wasn't much left. Karen never worked, so she could stay home with our kids. I had to work two jobs much of my married life.

Finally, a friend of mine said, *you should get into the real-estate business, in addition to teaching.* He thought I could sell, so I got my real-estate license in 1967.

I was very fortunate in the real-estate business. It was always my goal to try to save what I made in selling real estate. I sold one piece of ground for $95,000 in Olathe. My part of that commission was something like $7,000—I was making $5,000 a year teaching.

I got my broker's license in 1972 and moved into building houses on a part-time basis. My father-in-law had been a builder, built one or two at a time, a real small homebuilder. I built my first home and was going to move into it, when a real-estate lady came by and wanted to know if I'd sell it. So I sold the darn thing and slowly worked into the building business.

In 1974, '75, '76, and '77, I built a lot of houses part-time, over evenings and weekends. Karen and I would stay up all night paying the bills. I even painted a lot of my homes. It was very difficult, and I was slave labor, as I look back at it. I just worked so stupidly hard, which was not very smart. (*Being married with two young children and another on the way while working two jobs certainly created a stressful balancing act that wasn't always a success. Its toll on my marriage, coupled with other factors, would eventually lead to divorce, despite 40 some years of Karen and I trying to make it work.*)

I realized that I'd have to quit teaching or quit building. I was killing myself. (By the way, I was still coaching wrestling, and we were state champions that year!) I finally decided to quit teaching in 1977 and build homes full time. The last year I taught school, I built 50 houses working part-time. Worked my tail off.

In 1981, Merlyn Stuffings, a banker friend and partner in Olathe Ford, had 55 lots in Stagecoach Meadows, a subdivision in Olathe. He was going to sell them for $22,500. I bought them for just $10,000—he just wanted out. He sold them to me for nothing down, interest only—and the interest only due when I sold a lot!

It just so happened that Johnson County was offering a bond money program for first-time homebuyers. So I took the letter to the bank, and I got 50 loans, unbelievably enough. I built the houses on Merlyn's ground, in some cases, never paying for the lots until the house closed! I sold 50 homes the next year, all to first-time homebuyers. I made a lot of money. And I was able to do that despite interest rates going to 21% that year!

In total, I built about 700 or 800 houses, before I quit building full time in 1985. I had successfully made it through the recession of 1981, '82, '83. It was very, very difficult. When I quit teaching in 1977, interest rates were 6%. In 1979 they were 10%, and in 1980 they were 21%.

It was a rough start with a lot of ups and downs, but I fell in love with the building business. I found it exciting! Still, one of the first things I realized was how hard it was to find a safe and dependable place to build. You don't know which developer to trust. Is he financially strong? Is he reliable? Is it a safe place to build your home? There were (and still are) a lot of risks involved.

There were no big developments in the price range I was in, so I started looking for ground to buy myself. The first piece of ground I bought to develop was in Merriam, and I think it was 5 or 10 acres. It's still there today! I sold the house off the land, and then built my own homes around it.

I also did a lot of options. I could get someone to give me an option on a property—$1,000 or $500— and I would go sell it and make the extra money myself. I did several of those little deals where I bought 5 acres and had a house on it. Five acres would sell for $50,000. I would sell the house and one acre off for $50,000 to $55,000 and keep 4 acres. I developed an eye for how to make money, because I didn't have any money. No one has ever co-signed a note for me, so I had to look at ways to figure options or a low down payment or a place where I could buy something and sell something off.

At one point during those years, I bought 8 or 10 farms with houses and barns on each property. I would sell the houses and barns off and nearly get the ground almost free. It was really just a case of having to figure things out—how to swap and deal and trade.

I used my ingenuity, my gift, the gumption I had even as a child, to work for a better lifestyle. They used to tease me at Shawnee Mission West that I carried two quarters in my pocket, and I would rub them and rub them. They would say, *"What are you doing Darol?"*

I told them, "Someday I'm going to look in my pocket, and I'll find three quarters. If I rub them hard enough, there will be three someday!"

I gradually worked myself to buying bigger pieces of ground. That way I had time to build in one spot without constantly driving around looking for someplace new to build.

It dawned on me during the process that there was a need for a developer to make a real commitment to the homeowner *and* to the builders. I wanted to be the person who others could trust for a successful building experience. So I created Rodrock Development. "Building Better Communities" became our motto, and it was something I always did my best to stand behind. We focused on protected values—doing more than just building lots, but helping homeowners maintain or even improve the value of their homes with features like stone pillars, fountains, paved walking trails, playgrounds, pools, and parks.

I also started the Rodrock Development Moms' Council. The Council, which is run by residents, plans a slew of family-friendly activities, including spring egg hunts, Memorial Day pool-opening parties, July 4th bike-a-thons, outdoor movie nights, and pumpkin-carving contests. But the favorite tradition is in December, with holiday hayrides—complete with huge draft horses pulling wagons down decorated streets—and caroling, hot chocolate, and a visit from Santa himself.

These gatherings help new neighbors have fun, but they also build a strong sense of community and help provide families, and importantly children, a safe place to grow up. My goal has always been to make a community feel like a small town to people.

I figured out I could buy ground and provide a truly one-of-a-kind opportunity for builders, and they would come to me to purchase lots. And, in turn, homebuyers bought their homes in a Rodrock Development.

That's not to say it's always been easy. It was really hard in the 1980s and here again in the most recent real-estate bubble burst. Still, we had a run where we kept buying ground, and I kept looking for opportunities. Sometimes we had two to three subdivisions in competition with each other, so I had to make sure we separated the location, the product line, the name, and the community amenity package so each community would be unique.

To date, we've developed some 87 communities in Johnson County, making me the owner of one of the largest residential real-estate development companies in Kansas. There are nearly 30,000 people living in our communities. I have the privilege of building family-friendly communities where kids can grow up in beautiful homes with a sense of nurturing and belonging—something I never had as a child.

I've been blessed with a multi-million-dollar business. It's incredible that a little boy who grew up searching for a home to call his own now has the opportunity to create warm and welcoming communities for thousands of others. My work is filled with purpose for me, and I'm so grateful after all these years to do a job that I love—one that I feel makes a difference in my community and hopefully have a ripple effect in the world. By our estimates, Rodrock Development has generated more than $11 billion dollars into the local economy. Sometimes that's still hard for me to wrap my head around!

Obviously, I've come a long way financially since Little Darol searched for pop bottles for a coveted 10 cents. But in truth, I don't know that people ever feel financially comfortable. There's always a bit of fear lurking, a shadow of the old days of hunger and desperation. But my success allowed me to splurge on horses and cows. At one time I had 250 head of horses. (I'll admit, I didn't need that many! I just love horses!) I even owned a cowherd—but then my heart went bad, and I had to quit. Today I own just 20 horses, with two of our studs among the top 10 Western Pleasure horses in the nation.

Still, when it came to homes, cars, and vacation homes, I used my real-estate expertise. I traded for my vacation house on the oceanfront in Florida—*for free*! My good friend Bob Joy and I did a lot of real-estate deals together. We had deals in Wickenburg, Cave Creek, and Scottsdale, Ariz., and even in Shawnee, Kan. And I had a deal where I was able to make enough money to trade, tax free, through a 1099 tax-free exchange, for this Florida home that I love. Even my farms were bought at a bargain. Little Darol's sharp eye for a deal is still strong to this day.

I've never been driven by the desire to make more money, though. I've just always had the goal to do the very best I can, in whatever I try. And that has led to financial success in business.

Do I consider myself, personally, to be a successful person? Yes, I can say that I do. But not for the reasons many people would think. I believe there are countless definitions of "success," and we all have our own personal understanding of what that is for ourselves. For me, success is trying my hardest, and that's what I've done. It's about knowing I have given it my all, in both business and *in life*.

Darol coaching his wrestling team at Shawnee Mission West, in 1975. The team took 2nd place in State that year.

Darol and happy homeowners in 2013 in his development,
Stonebridge Meadows.

Darol and Rodrock Development residents at the Moms' Council
Holiday Hay Ride in the mid-90's.

10

THE COMPANY I KEEP
Taking care of people,
taking care of business

When I'm asked the "secret" to my business success, I know there are many factors involved. But I do believe that much of it comes from doing all I can to be wise in my choices, using my God-given creativity to solve problems, keeping my dealings honest, and treating people as I would want them to treat me. There are principals here I've believed from the beginning, some I've learned along the way, and others I'm discovering even today.

People are often surprised when I tell them I've always had only 3 to 5 employees. That's a lot of work for a few folks—more than a $100 million worth of business. How do we make it happen?

There are two simple rules in business that I live by every day:

1. Take in more than you spend. (That sounds pretty simple, doesn't it?)

2. The business of being in business is about people—not just about the trade.

The first rule sounds pretty obvious, but it's amazing how many businesses struggle with that simple principal: *Take in more than you spend.* People simply aren't aware of how much things cost sometimes. They don't have a good financial system and are often unable to stick with a realistic budget (if they have a budget at all!). They end up spending more than they take in, and their businesses fail.

For instance, in my homebuilding business, if I tell you I can build your house for $500,000, but I'm off on my numbers, I still have to build it for that amount. That's what we agreed upon. If I don't calculate correctly, then I end up going over budget. My company has to make up for that miscalculation, and we start to lose money quickly. So I have to have a solid, well-informed estimate upfront about how much we're going to spend on a home. It takes time and resources to lay a solid financial foundation for a company. It takes knowledgeable employees who can help make good decisions. And when something isn't working—maybe the economy changes or the business dynamics change—we need to make the necessary adjustments to ensure that we are always taking in more than we spend.

My second business rule is what I believe has truly set my company apart for all these years: *The business of being in business is about people—not just about the trade.* I always say I never made a nickel off a piece of ground. I only make a nickel when people *buy* the piece of ground.

Most certainly we have to know our trade. We have to know horse training, car sales, or a grocery business...whatever it is. But the bottom line is that it's about how we treat people. The money comes from offering a satisfactory product and taking care of your customer. Treat them how you'd want to be treated, and everything will fall into place.

People know if they are in a Darol Rodrock community, they're going to be taken care of. I've surrounded myself with people I can trust in my company—people who have integrity, no matter what the circumstance. I remind them, "In this business, we're all depending on each other. If you don't do your job right, the next guy can't do his job right." I've worked with the same employees and subcontractors for years and years—even decades. We honor one another, and we respect the people we serve.

I don't care what happens, or how unreasonable a person is being, my employees and I will treat them courteously. We try to put ourselves in their position and ask, *"Is this the way I'd want to be treated in a business climate myself?"*

In the construction business, there are always repairs that need to be made. We, as a company, are only bound to fix certain things for homeowners within a certain time period. However, in my company, I've gone back three or four years to make things right. In the goodwill of business and taking care of people, I think it's wise to spend a little money to make sure the customer is satisfied. It's what I call a *"short-term decision with a long-term effect."*

Say someone asks me to take care of something and I quickly say "no" without much consideration. Later, I realize I could've just as easily said "yes," put forth the little extra effort to fix the problem, and gained the lifelong trust of a customer. I learned a long time ago that what people think of me gets there long before I ever walk through the door. Having a trusted reputation is priceless. This is why I've always kept my financial books open. It's the honest thing to do, and that's who I want to be. It may also explain why in more than four decades of business, I've never been involved in a business lawsuit—never suing another and never having a suit filed against me.

In the long run, my goal isn't having more and more money anyway. It's doing a good job, maintaining integrity, sustaining a profitable business, and being able to move forward with confidence. I've always worked hard because I had to. And even if I make more money today, it isn't any more important to me. For me, it's never been the focus. Instead, it's always been about treating people right.

Think about this: What does it mean if I make a lot of money? Does it mean I've worked harder than you have? I'm luckier than you? I deserve it more? Here's what I think: Money measures whether or not I'm doing a good job and making the right decisions. Period. I've always told people, "Focus on doing things right, and the money will come."

I've tried to do things the right way all my life, as best I can. That's where I believe my financial success has come from. Not from being tightfisted, or clever, or from undermining the other guy to get more than he does. I realize that money has allowed me some wonderful opportunities in life, but it's not even close to what matters most to me.

How much money I make is not going to change who I am. I'll still be drivin' my Ford pickup truck, wearin' my boots and jeans, like always. To me, doing well financially just means I'm taking care of people. And if the money isn't there, then that's a good gauge for me—means I'm not doing something right. Always remember that, whatever field you're in.

Here's a story to illustrate my point about integrity: A few years ago, I was following news reports about two major U.S. car manufacturers. They had become aware of a potentially dangerous problem with the ignition on one of their models. It was something that would've cost them about 17 cents to fix per car, but they chose not to address it. Even when people were killed as a result, they still refused to acknowledge the problem to the public, knowing they'd lose money. They went 12 years without doing anything about it—figured out a gimmick to get away with it—and that problem killed many people.

I'm appalled that any person anywhere would think that money is more important than the life of a human being. What if it was the president of that company's son or daughter who was killed? Wonder if that would have changed their perspective.

I firmly believe that every life has equal value. Bill Gates' life is not worth more than mine. He has more money, but his life is not worth more. Is a homeless foster child's life worth as much as mine? Oh, yes. After all, I *was* that homeless foster child, and I feel like my life is valuable and rewarding to me and the people I serve.

You don't measure a man's net worth with his mo..cy. *Our net worth is who we are as people.*

And this is where I come back to what matters most: *The business of being in business is about people.* What we do for people, say to people, and how we take care of people makes all the difference in the world. I don't care what your trade is. Take sports management, for example. The business of being in baseball is not about getting the right pitcher. It's about filling a stadium with people. You've got to get people who want to come watch your team play. You can have the best players in the world, but what's the use if you've chased all the people away with bad business? If the people in your company are disrespectful to the customer who comes in the door, it doesn't matter how great your stadium is.

There's one very important piece to this puzzle that not every company possesses. Most businesses know *what* they're making and *how* to make it. But someone like Steve Jobs was successful because he had a "why" in the middle of the bull's-eye. He knew *why* he was making what he made. He wanted to change the way people communicate with each other. I remember him saying that "anyone can create a phone, but we want to change the world with our phone!" I believe the secret to all success is the "why." I can put streets and sewers in, build monuments—but it's *why* I do these things that makes all the difference. It's to serve the people who live there. I often encourage people to ask themselves, "Why am I doing what I'm doing? Why am I here, doing this work in the world?"

Prosperity isn't just a result of working harder or being smarter. I believe it's a gift we're given to share with the world. I've been given a great gift to bring families together. That's what my business is about to me. I create communities that feel like small towns, where moms and dads are able, and encouraged, to connect with their children. It's a genuine need of mine to help foster that connection—it's something I obviously never had growing up. *I want to help them build memories.*

Because that's my "why," every choice I make in my business goes through that filter. It's why I created the Moms' Council—something Rodrock communities are known for. It helps build a sense of community within my neighborhoods and fosters friendships and healthy families.

I'll never forget the time I watched a dad get off the horse-drawn wagon with his little 3-year-old son during a holiday celebration some 30 years ago sponsored by our Moms' Council. Stocking cap pulled down, runny nose—it was freezing cold that night. But that little boy had a smile as wide as a barn, and so did his dad. I remember thinking what I wouldn't give to have my dad take me on that ride. It meant so much to me, and I'm so proud that God put me in that position.

Sure, I don't have to do these things to run a successful business. I have the resources to build beautiful homes and leave it at that, but I'm driven to do more because I can—because I have the opportunity to create an atmosphere where families can strengthen their relationships and make memories that last forever. There's nothing to buying ground and putting streets in. But to create a true community—that's what makes all the difference for me. That's my "why."

And the "why" of my business isn't just found in the large communities I build. It's found in the small community of people that help run my company. I believe that every employee deserves to be valued and treated with respect, and our small staff is like family to me.

We have wonderful relationships, laughing together and sharing our lives. I know their stories, love their families, and we enjoy a mutual trust that makes work a great place to be. I give my people total flexibility. Never had a time clock. I pay them as much or more than they could make anyplace else in this county and give them as much freedom as I can if they'll do their jobs. I love my own freedom, so why wouldn't they love theirs? "Just take care of my business," I tell them. My expectations are clear.

I often joke I'm the worst boss in the world. Some bosses think they own their employees. But I don't think about them as employees; I just think about them as friends who work with me.

And I don't believe in firing people. I think "fired" is a degrading term, and I never use it. I tell my employees that if they want to leave me for another job, just tell me, and I'll do the best I can to help them get their next job.

Of course there have been a few occasions when I've had to ask an employee to leave. When that happens, I tell them I believe one of three things is going on. It's likely you're not doing your job because:

#1 You're not qualified. I may have hired you for a position that I thought you were qualified for, but it turns out you really didn't understand all the dynamics of that position.

#2 You're overworked. It's possible that when I hired you I thought we'd have a certain amount of work, and now we've gotten really busy. Maybe you've become so overwhelmed you just can't do the work.

#3 Maybe you just don't care about the job. Once you got into the job, you decided you just don't care about it.

After sharing these possibilities, I tell the person,

"I want to understand which of these three is going on for you. If we determine this isn't the right fit for you, let me help you find a job—a job where you want to be, a job you're excited about, qualified for, where you can do good work and won't feel stressed out and rundown." I want my employees to come to work full of energy and enthusiasm and without stress.

If someone comes to work every day with stress, they're not happy, and we can all feel it. We sense each other's energy—it's just the way we're wired. We share what we're feeling with one another, whether we realize it or not.

So the first thing to do when it's not working out is to accept the fact that there's an issue. Then, let's fix it together, or let me help you find something else. I'll recommend you to someone else. I'll help your potential employers understand why we weren't a good fit for each other. I won't cut you down, judge you, or sabotage your ability to get a good job in the future. I just want to encourage you and lift you up.

However, if we ignore the fact that there's an issue and don't address it, then it will most likely grow and eventually overwhelm both of us.

That's why I think it's important to keep this little saying close at hand: ***Stop a snowball before it becomes an avalanche***.

Whether it's our workplace, our homes, our

personal relationships, or some other area of our lives, we've all had these kinds of difficult situations come up. Often, they start fairly small (and maybe even seem "harmless" at first) but if we aren't careful, they'll grow a lot bigger, a lot quicker than we realize.

When people are facing problems, I often ask them: "How do you stop an avalanche?" They kind of chuckle at that. "A snowball is manageable, but once an avalanche starts, it can bury you."

I see challenging situations in life as snowballs. When I become aware of a difficulty, I can choose to identify it and do something about it, or I can do what a lot of people do—just ignore it. Put it off for another day until it finally becomes too big to handle. People allow a problem to get rolling, and then it gets big, and next thing they know it's burying their company, their marriage, and their life. I've certainly ignored my share of situations in my life and learned the value of this saying the hard way—especially in the business world!

We can prevent so much difficulty in our lives if we remember to address issues and talk about them—even seemingly minor ones—right away. Don't run away from them. It takes courage to see an issue for what it is. Recognize it. Stop it if you can, or at least start fixing it. Take steps right away, or it'll bury you sooner or later.

And lastly, remember that a little up-front preparation and strategic thinking can go a long way in helping us avoid some challenges altogether. I believe that the more we come to understand and learn about our trade, the more roadblocks we'll avoid and the more vision we'll develop. We can start to see possibilities that others can't.

Darol and his real-estate team in 1994, at Darol's 50th birthday party.

Darol and his General Manager, Tom Langhafer, walking the property of his Sundance Ridge community in 2017.

OUT OF THE SHADOW

§

When people learn about my past, they often ask how I got from there to where I am today. I hope that this book will be the answer to that question, and I believe it may be the most important thing I'll ever share in my life. While the story of my past—and yours—matters greatly, the story of our lives today matters infinitely more. Our past will always be a part of who we are, but it does not have to define us or limit us!

This is why, through the years, I've created a lot of little truths I live by. My beliefs developed out of my need to make sense of the world after the chaos of my childhood. I needed something to hold onto every day, because I felt so lost for so long. I needed to know there was some purpose in my life, some meaning…a reason to get up every morning and keep living and loving. You see, I lived in a great shadow for most of my life: the shadow of my past. And over time, my sayings became like little points of light that guided me through that darkness…

§

OUT OF THE SHADOW

11

OUT OF THE SHADOWS

Learning to live in the light of this day

One evening, while landing in an airplane, the sun was in just the right place, and I could see the shadow of my plane as we landed. As I looked out at the dark shape formed on the ground, a thought went through my mind: Am I in that shadow? I realized I had to be, and it dawned on me that many people, including myself, are living in a shadow like that in some way. It covers our bodies, our emotions, our spirits—and we are never able to truly see ourselves apart from that shadow.

Here's what I think happens: We all experience relationships, and sometimes things occur in these interactions that cast a shadow over us. Maybe it's abuse—sexual, physical, emotional—maybe it's pressure from our families to be a certain way or a romantic relationship where one person expects too much of the other. Whatever it is, we often carry the resulting feelings of abuse, neglect, rejection, isolation, guilt, fear, or resentment for the remainder of our lives. These are the things that keep us from lifting ourselves up into the light, into the glory that's available for us to live in each moment.

I believe virtually everyone has experienced some sort of shadow. It may not be from a traumatic childhood. Sometimes shadows are cast later in life by people who try to cut us down due to their own insecurities. Even as an adult, I lived in the shadow of people who were sarcastic and mean spirited.

But at some point in my life, I took a look in the mirror and said, "I've been making decisions *not* because of who I am, but because of who others have *told* me I am." I realized I'd been living in a dark place for a long time—one that prevented me from fulfilling my purpose. And as I looked around, I saw others struggling with that darkness, too. There are so many ways this can happen.

Think of a married woman who's abused by a

man, and then one day he leaves her with two kids and no money. She says, "I'll never marry again. I'll never be with a man, because that's what men do." So she lives in the shadow of her past marriage, never able to share the gifts she could offer to one who would truly love and take care of her.

And what about a father who overwhelms his son with his expectations? The son knows he can never be what his dad wants him to be. Or maybe he has a brother or sister who is so successful he feels like he could never accomplish as much as they have, so he doesn't even try.

I talked with a friend the other day whose dad was a strict disciplinarian—never complimented or encouraged her. He criticized everything she did. He cast a shadow over her. She felt she could never do anything right, never felt his love, so she just gave up trying.

Often people dealing with alcoholism, prostitution, or drug addictions have made choices about how to live their lives due to the impact of their shadow. They walk around weighed down by a sense that *I'm not good enough... I've made mistakes...*

When we feel that constant sense of guilt about what's been done, we may become afraid to leave our comfort zones anymore, fearful that we'll never gain enough confidence to make the right decisions. So many of us have held ourselves back from exploring the possibilities in life, the opportunities to be creative and productive and to fulfill our purpose, because we can't bear the thought of feeling like we never get anything right. So we don't even take the chance.

However, it doesn't have to be that way. When we finally become aware of the shadow we live in and stop denying it, then we are free to explore beyond it, to examine ourselves, and experience the fullness of life.

I'd like to think that God wouldn't want us to waste the precious gift of life being lost in the darkness. As the Bible says, "Don't hide your light under a bushel basket." We are each like a star that sparkles. We all have a way to light up the world with our own unique existence. We've got to let the radiance of that light shine! There's brilliance to our personalities and souls that's reflected in our bodies as we reach out, touch, and smile—as we lift up, encourage, and support those around us.

I tried to shine in my own way by not "buying" what my mother and dad tried to sell me when I was little. They'd tell me I was no good, worthless, not wanted—and a lot of people who hear that kind of thing will buy it. They'll take it into their soul and live with it the rest of their lives. They'll incorporate it into their thinking and let it hold them back forever. Some people will get lost in the shadow and never find their way out.

If we want to be free of the past, we must move forward into the light, expressing our true selves—no matter what it takes. I understand how difficult this can be. It's a tremendous challenge to avoid the kind of darkness that could eclipse the rest of your life.

And not only that, but it's important we make a conscious effort to avoid *casting shadows on others*. When we have been kept down for so long, we can easily pass that darkness along. If we aren't careful, the words that come out of our mouths, meaningful or not, intended or not, can affect the way people feel about themselves: *You're not very creative, are ya? You're sure a slow reader. You're not a very good dancer. It's your fault. Why do you keep making the same mistake? Can't you do anything right?*

For a child, or even an adult, those words can darken our lives with insecurity. We may lose our confidence, our ability to cope, and our assuredness that we were born into this world to shine in our own unique way.

The challenge is to discover ourselves—who we really are meant to be—in the light and not let the shadow of the past hold us back. Find joy in that challenge, and be grateful you can say *I won't live in that darkness anymore!* I want to encourage everybody to believe that no matter how dark our shadows are, there's hope for us all...we *can* live in the light!

But first of all we must recognize the shadow is real. Be aware that the things of the past still affect our lives today, but know without question that we each have the potential to live a life of brilliance.

I spent far too long feeling the weight of my own personal shadow. So I'm learning to express myself and walk out into the light, to be who I was meant to be and to serve others! Part of that process is the writing of this book. I pray what I share in these pages will resonate with you, wherever you are on *your* journey, so we can learn to walk in freedom together.

Darol in 1948 in Iola, Kan.

OUT OF THE SHADOW

12

THE PAIN WE SHARE

Compassion for ourselves...and each other

There are few things that cut me to my core like seeing people who are hurting. I believe no matter what any of us have been through, everyone's pain is equal; the pain of my past is no greater or less than yours. What I've been through can never be compared to what you've been through, because we all have our own journey to take, our own unique challenges to face. We each have something to overcome, and it doesn't make any difference how much of that something there is. Young, old, rich, poor, black, white—we've all had thoughts like, "There's no hope. Things are never going to change, never going to work out."

A lot of our issues relate to what our parents or others in life did or didn't do to us, what they said or didn't say. They may have beat us, abandoned us, sexually or physically abused us, cut us down with their words or just simply didn't encourage us when we felt we needed it. Some set expectations we could never meet; others destroyed the aspirations we had for our lives.

I can't say this often enough: What happened to me in the past doesn't have to affect the way I live my life today. I've chosen to stop believing the past ruined my life. I don't have to live in that shadow anymore. I want to live in the light of this glorious moment! I've had to encourage myself to see things differently, to understand that it's not what I went through—it's the way I see what I went through. I need to acknowledge that it was really, really tough for the child I was—the child who still lives in me today. I need to know I am safe now, and that I have the freedom to choose the way I feel about my life. I can offer myself all the love and compassion I need. In fact, I've learned the powerful truth that you can't give away what you don't have. The more compassion I have for myself, the more I have to offer other people. If I am filled with anger or bitterness, that's what I give away. If I'm filled with love and peace, that's what I give away.

As I understand and begin to heal from my own pain, I have the ability to sense the hidden pain in others. I can help them begin to heal, too. It is only when I compare myself—when I assume my pain is worse than that of other people and become centered on myself—that I no longer recognize pain in the other person. When I focus on my pain, I'm not aware of yours. The more I focus on you, the more I'll be able to help you heal, and somehow that lifts us both up.

And what's the most important thing about our challenges? We are facing them and overcoming them. We must always work to overcome them! It isn't like, *We got it! Finally. It's gone forever! Whew!* The challenges will always be a part of our history, and we must be aware each day that we can overcome rejection, isolation, loneliness, disappointment, and fear...whatever life brings our way. I often hear people say, "God won't give us anything we can't handle."

I don't believe God gives us any of those difficult things—pain, fear, rejection, loneliness, anger. But I *am* convinced that God has given me the power to overcome anything and the strength to live every day of my life to the fullest.

I believe it isn't how high this mountain is in my life or yours. It's the fact we see one at all. The Bible says the fruit of a mustard seed can move mountains:

"...Truly I tell you, if you have faith as small as a

mustard seed, you can say to this mountain, 'Move from here to there,' and it will move. Nothing will be impossible for you." [Matthew 17:20]

But I see things differently. I refuse to acknowledge that there's a mountain at all. I believe that when we have faith, there are no mountains. Instead we have opportunity. And when viewed that way, there's no need to fear or worry.

We may come to the point where we don't even see a mountain anymore. That's freedom. But no matter where we find ourselves on the journey today, let's meet each other where we are and help one another along the way.

*Beverly, Darol, Donnie, and Barbara in1951,
the first time they entered the orphanage.*

*Darol, Beverly, Barbara, and Donnie in 1954,
the second time they entered the orphanage.*

OUT OF THE SHADOW

13

REFUSING TO BE A VICTIM

Freedom from the past, joy in the present, hope for the future

If we're going to live in the light of truth, we must let go of this toxic belief: *I am a victim.* Nothing ensures that you stay trapped inside the darkness of your past like having a victim mentality. Don't get me wrong—it's a tempting thought, particularly for those of us who've experienced significant trauma in the past. Choosing to *not* see yourself as a victim is one of the hardest things to do, especially for someone who's been rejected, abandoned, or suffered some kind of discrimination.

Being a victim comes from feeling like life just hasn't been fair. Maybe you didn't get the right amount of something; you were born into poverty; you didn't have the best set of parents, or opportunities, or abilities. Maybe you feel like a brother or sister was favored more. Somehow things in your life didn't work out so you could get what the next guy did.

If we constantly focus on what we *don't* have instead of what we *do,* we may end up living a life marked with jealously, anger, and bitterness. We're likely to withdraw from the world, strike out, and hurt the people we blame for "ruining our lives," or even hurt someone else. Every one of these missteps can trap us in the past and keep us cowering in the shadows of what we want—and *need*—to leave behind.

I know how tempting it can be to live that way. I understand the feeling of being "short-changed" and living with a constant sense of loneliness. I understand what it means to have parents who don't love you, or you *think* don't love you. It's a daily fight to say, *I will never be a victim. I'm going to rise above the past; rise above the experience that life's not fair. I'm going to rise above all of it and walk out of the shadow.*

Prisons are full of men and women who are angry because they felt short-changed in life. Many are consumed with resentment.

I gave a talk to a group of recovering addicts one night about a story I'd seen on TV that really impacted me. It was a documentary on the Pennsylvania State prison. The interviewer asked several inmates, "How did you get here? What did you do?"

And there was this angry-looking, bald-headed guy who answered: "I hated my f------ mama. She'd tie me and my brother to a tree, beat us, and leave us there all night...cold nights, bleeding from where she beat us. I hated her and wanted to kill her. But she died before I could do it."

"Then why are you in prison today?" the interviewer asked.

And the man answered through clenched teeth, "Those five women I killed took the place of my mama."

He killed five women, because he was angry about something his mother did. His violence stemmed from the fact that all his life he'd seen himself as a victim. If he'd only realized he could have given it to God and found a life of love, peace, and joy instead of anger, fear, and resentment. He could have *given* something to the world, but he chose instead to *take* something from it. Five women are dead today, because he never overcame his anger.

After I shared that story, a man came up, tears running down his face.

"Darol," he said, "you saved my life tonight. I was gonna kill my girlfriend and my best friend and then kill myself. They're messing around with each other, and I can't take it."

He showed me the gun on his side. He said, "I'm going to pray for myself, so I can be peaceful the rest of my life."

And I believe his life took a very different turn. He found some direction, has a successful business now, and truly knows the Lord.

No matter who we are or what we've been through, *we can always choose to rise above the victim mentality*. But in order to do so, we must first become aware of what we're thinking—not just today, but every day.

When we start having thoughts like: *I'm a victim...Nobody loves me...I'm not worthy...I shouldn't even be here...Life's not fair*, it affects our feelings. We feel frustrated and rejected, lonely and worthless. That's how we fall into the trap of hurting ourselves— and others.

As we become aware of what we're feeling, we need to take a step back and ask ourselves: What thought am I having that's causing me to want to do this? From where is that thought coming? And most importantly, what do I WANT to think instead? Remember, our bodies will always follow our thoughts. We may not realize we have a choice, but we do!

My mind controls everything about my life. The more I can be aware of what I'm thinking in any situation, the more present (and pleasant!) I can be. What happened in life happened. It's over. My thoughts do not have to be determined by my circumstances...past, present, or future.

People often ask me, "But Darol, what can I do to avoid getting caught in that trap of feeling sorry for myself? What do I do when I start to have those thoughts? I didn't even have a childhood like yours, and I still struggle with this!"

There are two main things I do to help myself avoid a "poor me" attitude:

1. Change my perspective.

2. Determine my own self-worth.

Changing my perspective: Today, when I find myself going down that "victim" path, I try to stop for a moment and remind myself to be grateful for what I have right now. We can all find something to be thankful for, can't we? Rather than being angry about what we don't have and what we want, we can take a moment to become aware of our many blessings.

One example from my own life is riding and working with cutting horses. That's something I dearly loved and always looked forward to. But because of several shoulder injuries, I can't ever ride again. I was so disappointed and angry when the doctor told me. I could easily hold onto those feelings—bitterness, frustration, maybe even resentment toward my friends who are still able to participate. Or I could choose to be thankful that I even had the chance to ride—had the pleasure of making so many friends, saw different places, experienced the thrill of winning.

Determining my own self-worth: The other thing I do to avoid becoming a "victim" is to decide that I will be the one to determine my self-worth. What you think of me, what the world thinks of me, even what my family or friends think of me—that does not have to determine what I think of myself. I can't control what others think on any given day. It's hard enough to control what I think most of the time!

Do you realize how many people hurt their spouse, their partner, or their children because they, themselves, feel worthless? They've let the world judge them and tell them who they are because of where they came from, what kind of job they do, or how much money they have or don't have. They carry around that sense of worthlessness, and it makes them feel powerless and angry. Those thoughts turn into actions, and pretty soon they've done something they could deeply regret.

Same with parenting. Our state of mind and our feelings about ourselves will often determine our course of action with our kids. I think there's not a parent alive who would say they don't love their children—even as they shake their baby in a moment of uncontrolled rage, beat their toddler, or humiliate their teenager. For most people, it isn't so much a lack of love as it is a complete lack of control of emotions. This may be rooted in the negative way they see themselves, their own feelings of powerlessness, and their lack of self-awareness. They don't think about what they're thinking, and once they act on those hidden thoughts, it's too late.

Now I want to be clear that I don't believe I have this whole thing figured out! I'm still developing my own self-worth. Still learning to pause for a moment and become aware of my thoughts. But I like that young boy, Little Darol, more all the time. I remind myself: He's a survivor! If he could whoop 'em as a child, I can whoop 'em today! If the child you were survived what you went through, the adult you are today can survive, too! You have freedom of thought that the child in you never had. And even if you didn't experience some kind of childhood trauma, you've been through challenges in your life, and you have survived. You have strength inside to draw from—and don't forget, you can win!

I'll end with a little story about a counselor friend I had for many years. His name was Bob Craft—one of those people placed in my life at just the right time. At that point in 1981, I was overcome with stress. Absolutely paralyzed with crushing anxiety. Several family members were severely ill and interest rates topped 21%, putting immense pressure on my business. Bob was an eccentric fellow who seemed almost larger than life. He was 6-foot, 4-inches tall, drove a '74 Cadillac convertible, and always had a cigar in his mouth. He'd show up to our counseling appointments in a 10-gallon hat, cowboy boots, and shorts! Bob was a Baptist minister for 28 years and chaplain of the Kansas City Chiefs football team for 15.

Bob had a gift for helping me look at my life differently—often in ways I hadn't thought of before. I'd tell him about all the things my parents did to me as a child, and he'd sit and listen awhile. Then he'd ask an unexpected question. One day it was: "What did you get from your parents, Darol? They may have been abusive, may have been sarcastic and mean-spirited, beat you, but there has to be something they gave you that's helpful in your life?"

It hadn't occurred to me to consider that, and, as a

matter of fact, it made me mad that he even asked me the question.

"Your mom and dad were both married many times, right? Can you imagine how much energy that would take? Being married multiple times, and your dad being an alcoholic all his life? And having all those kids between the two of them? Wow, they had a lot of energy! The energy you have today is more than any man I've ever met. That's something they gave you, isn't it, Darol?" He'd smile. "Maybe you could be thankful for what they gave you."

What an eye-opener! You see, Bob wasn't dismissing my past, but he was helping me see that I can choose to see things differently today. What happened to that little boy happened. We all come from somewhere. We all experience circumstances that are sometimes beyond our control. But it's our personal responsibility to decide how we will see our lives and ourselves. We have the ability to respond in whatever way we choose. That is something that can never be taken away from us. The more we enjoy that freedom, the less we'll fall into the trap of becoming a victim, and the stronger we will become!

Darol after his 1st place win at the 2007 N.C.H.A. Superstakes.

Darol cutting at the N.C.H.A. Futurity Show, where he won 4th place out of 296 entries. This was the first time he rode cutting horses, and he was 62 years old.

Darol and Dr. Bob Craft, his counselor and lifelong friend.

14

INEQUITY & DISADVANTAGE

Learning to rise above it all

My passion for helping people escape the shadow of victimhood comes from the years I spent in their shoes. Whether it's poverty or abuse, my heart breaks for those precious souls who feel their lives are worthless. They need to hear from someone who **has** felt their pain that they are valued, that they have unique and important gifts to share with the world, and that they don't have to continue to carry the weight of the hateful, belittling words and actions of others.

When I'm invited to speak in churches, schools, and other organizations, I want these folks to see me not as an old successful white man, but as someone who's been in their shoes and felt the pain and rejection that many of them feel. I tell them, "I know what it means to have head lice so bad nobody wants to be your friend, to have clothes so dirty and smelly you're embarrassed to go to school because no one wants to be near you. I know what it is to be 'from the wrong side of town.' The other kids would call me 'white trash.' I know what it means to be looked down on because your dad is in prison. That's what prejudice feels like, and you are not alone in that feeling."

Like many kids today, I felt like I could never be successful because of who I was, the family I was born into, where I came from. My dad was an ex-convict. My mother was barely surviving. I had no roots to speak of—no strong foundation to build upon. When I look back on my childhood, I truly wonder how I made it. Rehashing my history is emotionally draining, but I share my stories in hopes that children experiencing some of this now will know I truly understand their pain. And not only that, but there is hope for anyone in any circumstance, no matter where you are today.

We've all seen kids who're obviously struggling at

home. Maybe their family is barely making ends meet. Maybe Mom works all night, Dad lost his job, or they've ended up in foster care, and it isn't a good situation. Maybe they come to school looking tired and unkempt, or you pass them on the street walking with their head down—worn-out clothes, no coat. They're right here among us, and they just need someone to reach out a helping hand.

During our time in Humboldt, Kan., we had a long, cold walk to school in the winter months, and we had no coats. It was a dreadful feeling to wake up in the morning knowing how far we'd have to go in the bitter cold. I have compassion for the little kids we were, hunched over against the onslaught of snow, wind, and rain. Thankfully, our teachers eventually ended up providing coats for us that winter. We were so grateful, and I never forgot their generosity.

There was one small source of heat at home during that terrible winter—the gas stove that stood in the living room. It was the only warm spot to be found in the entire house. On cold winter nights, we'd crowd in as close as we could to that little stove. Maxine would fix sugar popcorn, one of the only things I remember her actually enjoying. We'd lie there on the floor and listen to Hank Williams and Ernest Tubb and all those old singers in front of a little brown radio. For just a moment we felt warm and happy. But bedtime brought a desperate, sinking feeling. We knew we were headed to a cold bedroom where we'd have to lay on damp sheets reeking of urine.

Through the years, I've learned that when you're living like that, in survival mode, all your energy and attention is focused on just getting your needs met. There isn't much opportunity to develop a sense of self-worth. When you've got nothing, it's easy to feel like you *are* nothing, and this world will confirm that in many ways.

I spoke awhile back to a group of foster kids and parents at Church of the Resurrection in Leawood, Kan. I walk in, and here I am this white-haired old man. I start talking and you can just see them thinking, *What's he got to say? What does* he *know?* Ten minutes into the talk, I could see their eyes start to follow me as I walked on the stage. One man wrote a letter afterward that said, "You captivated the kids that day. And I just can't find the words to say what you did for us parents."

I can give a powerful talk on poverty, violence, and abuse. You know why? Because I lived it.

I talked that day about how God has given us all gifts to share with the world. A little girl near the front raised her hand and said, "But, Mr. Rodrock, I don't think I have any gifts from God."

So I pulled her up on stage. "What's your name, dear?" I asked.

"Nancy," she said shyly.

I looked at the audience and said, "Let's say a little prayer for Nancy. Isn't it a shame that God didn't make her right and give her any gifts?"

She kind of giggled. I said, "Wait a minute, Nancy. Can you dance?"

"No."

"Can you sing?"

"No."

The list went on, and she kept saying, "No, no, no..."

"I didn't get any gifts, Mr. Rodrock."

"Well, you can talk pretty well," I told her.

"Oh, I'm a good talker," she said.

"Well there's something. And what are you going to be when you grow up?"

"Oh, I hope to be a school teacher."

"You mean you've got the gift to teach someone else something?" I raised my eyebrows. "Wait a minute, kids. We don't have to pray for any more gifts for Nancy. She can talk, and she can teach!"

I looked at her: "What we need to ask *you*, Nancy, is 'Are you going to use the gifts God gave you to the best of your ability? Do you have the courage to use those gifts to serve the Lord and serve others? Are you going to study, go to college, and become a teacher?'"

Her face lit up, and she nodded, *yes.*

You see, these kids need to know that everybody's got something to offer, something to be proud of and feel good about.

I talked to them about Jesus that day. Not the religious, clean-cut, good smellin' Jesus, but the real nitty-gritty Jesus who's been with me all my life. I told them, "You know somewhere I learned that Jesus walks with me, and He talks with me. And you know what? He told me one day that I am actually His *own*." Makes me smile just thinking about how that lost kid in me felt when someone finally said I belonged to them.

"Kids," I told them, "you'll never look back if you believe Jesus has taken your hand like that. You'll never, ever be alone again. You want to live the way your parents lived? You go right on. It's your choice. And you can live the rest of your life in that shadow they put over your head..."

"Or decide today to take another path. It's the difference between feeling like you're in chains all your life and being free. It's a choice you get to make. And guess what? *Nobody else can make that decision for you.*"

No matter what we are dealing with, we all have a

choice to make. Do I just continue down the path everyone else around me is taking? Or do I have the courage to make something of my life, no matter what other people believe about me or how they treat me?

When people face such unfairness, I encourage them to stop and ask themselves: "What truly matters most—what other people think of me, or what I think of myself?"

Your answer to this question plays a big part in shaping who you become. Will you let others determine your path in life with their beliefs about you, or will you chart your own course? Will you step out of the shadow of your past and into the light of possibility and freedom? We can choose to let it direct our lives, let it hold us down—or we can move past it. We can't control the beliefs of others, *but we can choose our own beliefs about ourselves.*

Darol speaking to foster-care youth at the annual Darol Rodrock Foundation Holiday Party in 2016, encouraging them to believe in themselves.

15

ANGER & VIOLENCE

Living through the chaos...
Choosing a path of peace

We must be aware of a dangerous obstacle in our quest to live our lives in the light of freedom. It's an emotion that can quickly fill us with darkness, and it can be a particular struggle for people who've dealt with discrimination and disadvantage in their pasts: *Anger.*

We all know that anger is a natural emotion. It's not something we should stuff down or try not to feel. In fact, the more we ignore it, the more it can overwhelm us—especially if we are carrying deep-rooted resentment and bitterness within. But what do we do when it comes up? (And it does come up in all of us at some point, whether we recognize it or not!) How can we avoid making life-altering mistakes while under its explosive influence? And most importantly, how do we avoid passing our anger issues on to our children?

When you grow up in an angry, violent atmosphere, you breathe in fear and uncertainty every day. When the adults who are supposed to nurture and protect you instead beat you (and each other) daily, it can feel like there's no one to trust, nowhere to go where you can feel safe. When you're 5, 6, and 7 years old and are being beaten by a parent, what are you going to do? Go to the police and say, *"My mama's beatin' me?"* It's so confusing. This is the person you depend on, whose love you're desperate for...this same person is hurting you, making you feel like you're bad, shameful, worthless, and you may even feel like it's your fault.

I wonder now as I look back, why didn't I tell someone about what was happening to me? I suppose it was because I felt trapped. There are kids today being beaten, abused, or raped, and that's how they feel. Being trapped has to be one of the worst experiences for a child. It can create intense anger, whether a child is aware of it or not. They may act it out or hold it in...but it's there. And even when they're no longer trapped, they're angry about all that time they *were.* They come out of an environment where they felt helpless, hopeless, defeated, maybe for years. They grow up angry and don't even know how to deal with—let alone *escape*—that feeling.

That's the atmosphere I was born into. The violence between my mother and father was part of our daily lives. To witness your parents screaming and hollering on the front porch, swinging at each other, having the police come—imagine what it does to a little child.

Even when my father had gone away to prison, he came home on parole and raped and beat my mother brutally. I remember my sister Beverly running into the bedroom, taking Donnie and me away to hide in the closet. She wanted to protect us from having to see something so horrific...and here Beverly was just a child herself.

One time in Iola, Kan., we followed a trail of blood through the house and found Maxine crumpled in our closet, unconscious. Whitford had beaten her and stuffed her in there—hit her so hard he broke her nose and knocked teeth right out of her head. We got towels and washrags and tried to clean her up. It was terrifying. We were sure she was dead.

And it wasn't just Whitford who was violent. Maxine had a pattern of marrying alcoholic, abusive men. She seemed to have an insatiable desire for male attention and could never settle down with just one, even though she was married five or six times.

I remember one of her husbands from our time in Iola. His name was Donald Ray, but we called him Did. He was 21 years old, to Maxine's 27. Did and his brother, Charlie, used to go out drinking with their buddies at night in an old abandoned building near where we lived. Being a curious kid, I tagged along. I'll bet there were a thousand pigeons in that old building, and once the guys got to drinking, they'd start catching those pigeons and biting their heads off. Each guy would take a turn, and the last one to gag was the winner. Even though it was funny to me at the time, here I was just a kid standing there taking this all in. I look back now and shake my head. It's just another example of the senseless violence I witnessed as a child.

One night, I came home to find Did throwing Maxine's small collection of records across the room at her as hard as he could—just firing them off like Frisbees. They were stuck in the wall everywhere. She was on the divan trying to get away from him, so I ran over and laid on top of her to try and protect her. It was strange to have that instinct to protect my mother, even though she was the one beating me night after night. They eventually divorced, and I never saw him again.

The incident that really shaped my understanding of our family's violent legacy happened in Garden City, Kan., at my Grandma and Grandpa Rodrock's house. My Grandma Rodrock was the first real loving connection I had in my life. Grandma taught me about gentleness and kindness, two things I never received from my own parents. She was special to me, and I believe somehow we needed each other at that time in our lives.

On this particular visit, when I was around 9 years old, Grandpa Rodrock was sitting at their kitchen table. He was an enormous man. Had huge hands like bear paws, and when he talked, that's how he sounded—like a big, growling bear. He was taking a bite of his supper and thought Grandma hadn't fixed something right, so he took one of those big paws and backhanded her as hard as he could. "BAM!" This 6-foot, 2-inch, 350-pound man just knocked her up against the wall.

She was a tiny lady, barely 5-feet tall. Blood was everywhere. I was totally stunned. I'd never seen Grandpa hit my Grandma before.

I ran over to try and help her up. Her nose was bleeding, and she was crying. Grandpa growled, "Ruth, I told you what I wanted!" Of course, he had been drinking.

I helped Grandma rise up to her elbow. She took a deep breath and said slowly and clearly: "If you ever hit me again, Walter Rodrock, I'll stab you with a butcher knife while you're sleepin'."

I never saw him hit her again. Maybe he believed her. I sure did.

The entire episode scared me to death. Years later, Maxine told me Grandma was so embarrassed and angry that he'd hit her in front of me, it gave her the courage to rise up and say, "Enough!" Looking back, I'm proud of her for being so brave.

Seeing that kind of violence in their home made me realize where my dad got it. His father beat his mother, so he beat his own wife. And that's how it happens in families, generation after generation, until somebody finally breaks the chain, until somebody steps away from the darkness of the past.

Would I be the one to do it? There's no question I absorbed much of the anger and violence I experienced, and as a child, emotional outbursts were a natural reaction. I didn't know any other way to be.

I remember an episode from kindergarten—an example of the violent path I could've taken. Back in those days we had stick horses, toy horse heads on wooden broom handles. Mine was named "Trigger," and he had a palomino mane.

Well, there was a kid in my class who wanted my

stick horse. He was already on my bad side, because he was always razzing me about my dad being in prison. (I used to try and tell the kids that Whitford was a truck driver, and that's why he was always gone.) This boy stole Trigger one day at recess and started riding him around. I yanked that stick horse away from him and broke it over his head. That's how I'd learned to handle a situation. I didn't like someone? I just hit them: *BAM!*

When did I decide *not* to take that path? When did I decide to step out of that shadow? No matter how strong that feeling of anger was in me, I knew I wanted no part of the violence I grew up with. Even as a young man, I vowed not to carry on my father's legacy. Not only do I never want to hurt anyone, but also violence terrifies me to this day. I know what out-of-control anger can do to people. A person who has violent thoughts can do violent things. I'll remove myself from any situation that may involve physical conflict.

My brother, Donnie, is just the opposite. It's like he absorbed the violence he witnessed and experienced as a young boy. He was the sweetest, most harmless little guy you'd ever meet, but as he got older, he became a victim. He grew into the kind of person who'd walk up to you, tap you on the shoulder, and hit you as hard as he could in your face. We're not talking a playful little sucker punch. We're talking maybe he'd take your eye out or break your nose.

Donnie quit school when he was 14—got kicked out of the Pierceville, Kan., schools because he was so mean. He was involved in a fight at school and someone called the police. When the officer arrived, he reached out and got a hold of Donnie. Donnie punched him once and knocked him out cold. Hit him right in the nose! Needless to say, he was in some trouble after that. (*Sadly, Donnie has never truly escaped the shadows of his past, and his life has been aimless and marked with difficulty. I love and support him to this day.*)

And then there was me—a brawl was the last thing I ever looked for. I remember an incident in the Marysville High School halls that marked my last so-called "fight."

Back in the '60s, we had these narrow school hallways with big bathroom doors that opened out into them. Between classes, the halls would be crowded with kids rushing back and forth, and if you weren't paying attention, those doors could just about knock you out. Here I am, walking down the hallway, talking with my friends, and a fella named Tom comes busting out of the bathroom, knocking me right to the ground.

"Tom, what're you *doin'*?" I looked up at him.

"What if I'd been a teacher? Miss McMullen or somebody!?"

Think I must've embarrassed him, because before I knew it, *POW*! He popped me upside the head, made my ears ring.

"Okay, Tom. Let's talk this over..." I said, being the diplomat that I was. I started to get up and *BAM*! He hit me up the other side of the head!

Everybody was around saying, *"Get up! Get up, Darol!"* Nobody knew my past back then. Being in a fight was the last thing I wanted to do, so I wouldn't hit him back. I walked away.

Tom was a good guy, but anger could take him over at the drop of a hat. Many people have pent up frustration just beneath the surface like that. If they're not careful, it can turn into anger and full-blown rage in an instant. When that happens, people are past the ability to reason or think. They'll even kill each other, whether that's their intention or not. And there's no going back after something like that happens. You lose your mind for a moment and regret it for a lifetime. That's what I call a short-term decision with long-term consequences.

That's what my dad's life looked like: He could destroy a person in an instant. I saw him when I was 4 years old, again when I was 10, and the last time when I was 20. That was the year he did something I will never forget. One night at the KU fraternity, I heard, "Rocks, you got a phone call!" (Rocks was my nickname.)

I picked up the phone, and there was a voice I hadn't heard in years "This is Whitford, your dad," he said. "I want to see you."

It was the last voice I was expecting to hear.

"Why the hell do you want to see me now?" I asked. "What's going on?"

He said, "I'm your dad, and I messed up, and I'd like to see you."

So for whatever reason, I decided to give him a chance. I guess every boy somehow longs for a father's approval. I'd just gotten a brand new '64 Tempest from Lavon and Ray. I drove it to a place way out in western Kansas called Oakley—almost to Colorado. Met Whitford and his latest wife, Winnie, and her little girl. They were driving what we used to call a "love van" in those days—a little van you could sleep in.

Whitford was almost 50; Winnie was 34. She was a sweet gal—just delightful. Night and day difference between her and my mother. I remember thinking, *It's not my dad at all*! It's my *mother* who's been crazy as hell all this time! She's been lying about my dad!

It's true my father had a deceptive personality. He was likeable, charming—but you never saw him without a beer in his hand. He drank it like water. In fact, he drank two or three cases just in that one weekend. We fished together, and he told me how he'd missed us and made a mistake and that he'd love to be back in my life. And I kept thinking, *What's wrong with my mom? He's really a pretty nice guy.* Still, I was cautious.

We spent Saturday together, and Sunday by noon I was ready to go back. He said, "Hey, can you do me a favor? I have to go to Beatrice, Neb., and get some Electrolux parts." (He was a salesman at the time.) "Could you run Winnie and her daughter down to Grandma's in Garden City for me?" It was about 80 miles straight south. I agreed to drive them there, and then I'd go on back to school in Lawrence.

Well, on the way down there about 4 in the afternoon we had a blowout. Not just a flat tire, a total blowout—and I had no spare. I was a college kid, not thinking about spare tires and backup plans. In fact, I don't know to this day where we even got a tire, but somehow we found one from somebody. We got to Grandma's about 4:30 in the morning. I dropped Winnie off and drove on to Lawrence.

A few weeks later, Maxine called and said, "Well, what do you think of your no-good dad *now*?"

I said, "Well Maxine, I don't know *what* to think about him now. He seemed like a pretty nice guy."

She said, "Well I guess you heard about Winnie, didn't you?"

"No." I was confused.

"She's still in the hospital," Maxine said. "Whitford beat her so hard they don't know if she's going to live."

Apparently, when he'd heard about our delay that night, Whitford decided that we'd stopped somewhere and had an affair. He wouldn't believe we'd had car trouble. He broke her nose, her eye sockets, her ribs, broke the teeth out of her face. Beat her like a dog. Grandma and Grandpa had tried to stop him, but it was no use.

I didn't hear from my dad again. In 1989, my half-brother called. "Darol, this is Jack," he said. "Our dad died. We need your help."

"What do you need from me?" I asked.

"We need money to bury him," he told me.

"All that family out there, and you're telling me you don't have the money?" I asked.

"His body is in the morgue, and we need $400 for his burial," he said.

I ended up agreeing to bury him. After all, he was my dad. He wasn't a true father by any means, but he was my biological father, so I was going to make sure he was buried properly.

I drove all the way to Garden City, about a 7-hour

drive from Kansas City. I cried all the way, thinking about my family and our past. The funeral consisted of myself and just four other people, including the minister. Found out that Whitford had been living in a trailer in a junkyard; that's where his life ended.

Many people are likewise shocked to find out I supported Maxine until she died. I bought her a home and car, gave her money every month. People ask: *"Why would you* ever *consider helping her after all she did to you?"*

The truth is, at some point I decided I just didn't want to be angry with her anymore. To live with resentment is such a waste of precious energy. Through counseling, I learned to have compassion for Maxine—for the suffering she'd endured in her own life. I learned to not judge her for the mistakes I thought she made. After all, it was her life, and they were her choices. And she likely didn't have many good choices to choose from: There she was, in her late 20s with four kids she couldn't care for, living in poverty, beaten and abused, probably totally exhausted. I reminded her of the man she detested most, and she just poured a sense of hatred, hopelessness, and worthlessness into me. Maybe she would've done something different if she could've. Maybe she felt trapped too—paralyzed by her circumstances. We never did speak of what happened throughout my childhood, so I will never know.

Still, I've often had people ask me, "What made you overcome all this? What did you do to handle that kind of pain and despair and frustration? What made you different—kept you from becoming a victim and living a life of anger like so many people do?"

First of all, I have to say it's easy to be angry...so easy to start thinking, "Oh, poor Darol."

But I know one thing: I learned early on in my life that staying angry serves no purpose whatsoever for me. It doesn't make me think better, doesn't make me stronger, and doesn't help me succeed. In my experience, it just makes things worse. No matter what people do or say to me, being overcome with anger doesn't help anything. When we feel like we're not in control, we get angry, and then we really lose control! It's a vicious cycle.

And as it was for my dad, anger is destructive to the people who let it take over their lives. Our prisons are full of people who reacted when they were angry—struck out in a moment of rage, and now they're living to regret it.

I'm not saying my own ego doesn't take me to the edge at times. We've all experienced flashes of anger, whether we acted on them or not. I'll get upset over something, flare up and spout off my frustration, *but I'll never engage or attack the individual I'm upset with.*

That's the most important part. If there's a conversation to be had—an issue to address with someone—that can come later. First, I need to deal with the thoughts that are causing my anger, need to come back into balance—back into a place of peace where I can think clearly and without judgment. I've always had a saying: ***Never make a decision when you're high or when you're low.***

This can benefit us in our business lives, personal lives, relationships, conflict resolution—so many things. If we make a decision based on the emotion we're having at the moment, it can't be a well-thought-out decision. Say you're angry that an employee made a costly mistake. "You're fired!" you shout at him, and he walks out. You might have just let go of one of your best workers, only because you lost control of your emotions in an instant.

It's okay to feel anger; it's a natural emotion. I'm not going to punish myself for having angry thoughts. But I'm aware that it's not a time to follow through with an action I'll regret later. I want to choose a different path—I *get* to choose! And I've learned that staying angry is never the right choice. And even further, as I've gotten older, I've realized that it's not even worth getting angry in the first place.

We need to model this for kids today—to let them know that they *do* have a choice about how they react, no matter how powerful their feelings are in the moment. We spend so much time being concerned about their education, their career, and what the world would call their future "success." But if we don't take the time to help them understand what's going on inside themselves, it doesn't matter how successful they look on the outside. I believe the more inner awareness children have, the more purpose-filled lives they will be able to lead. They won't be tossed this way and that by their life circumstances; they will have a firm foundation to stand on. And what more could we hope for their lives—or ours—than that?

Darol's grandfather, Walter Rodrock, in 1945.

Grandma Rodrock and her grandkids in 1949.

Darol's father, Whitford, in 1940.

Grandma and Grandpa Rodrock in 1953.

OUT OF THE SHADOW

16

WHO CARES ABOUT KIDS

Hearing their hearts, inspiring their spirits

Imagine how we might impact younger generations with the message of managing anger. Instead of carrying the weight of anger and regret into adulthood, they can learn how to let go early on—how to avoid the darkness that has engulfed too many young lives. But how do we begin to help the children we care about to live in the light?

One by one.

Even the smallest act of kindness or moment of listening can change the course of a child's life—

especially those who are struggling.

Paul Tough, author of *How Children Succeed: Grit, Curiosity, and the Hidden Power of Character* (a book I highly recommend!), describes the effect of stress on the brain of a young child. "Children who grow up in stressful environments generally find it harder to concentrate, harder to sit still, harder to rebound from disappointments, and harder to follow directions. And that has a direct effect on their performance in school." (And, I would add, in life.) Even if they make it through school, these kids often end up out on their own with no life skills. We can't expect them to be successful if they don't have the tools they need.

Tough speaks of how our emotional stability is developed before we're 6 years old. Those early years are the foundation of our thinking, our temperament, and our personality. Who we are as small children is who we grow into. Without loving intervention, it can be difficult for children—in particular foster kids, abused kids, and abandoned kids—to become emotionally stable adults.

If a child never bonds with a parent or feels accepted and loved, it's very difficult to build relationships of trust, cooperation, and unity. These children can feel like they never "belong" to anything. After all, they didn't bond with or "belong" to their parents.

It's a little bit like a baby calf that loses its mother. It goes around to other cows, trying to steal milk. They kick it and butt it, chasing it off. Cows mostly take care of only their own calves, and eventually the orphan calf will die. It's a little bit that way for people. If children feel unloved or unwanted, they can die emotionally. They can struggle to bond with others and can feel isolated all their lives. Making children feel welcome and loved—and to not feel rejection at an early age—is crucial for their development of loving, trusting relationships.

What's more, we have to understand what children are carrying—both those who experience severe trauma and those who are dealing with typical childhood hurts and adolescent growing pains. There's a reason they say the things they say and do the things they do, but we have to tune into them to truly understand. I've often noticed that when children do something unacceptable—strike out, scream, disobey in some way—parents will punish their actions. I think we've probably all done it at one time or another to our children. Instead of asking ourselves *what thought made that child do that?*, we simply punish them without trying to understand the emotion the child is going through.

Here's one thing I firmly believe: ***You can't punish a child into stopping what he's thinking.*** You can punish his actions, and that may stop what he's doing at the moment, but he'll still have those thoughts of rejection, loneliness, whatever he's feeling. Usually a child is not even aware of what he's thinking. But something in his mind is behind his actions—a word, a feeling, a look from someone, and BOOM, he reacts! Then he's punished for it, and the cycle continues.

It's true; we can't control the thoughts of children. But we can take the time to understand them. We can let them know we're listening, and we can help them change their thoughts and learn to control their actions.

Even as adults, we know that our actions follow our thoughts, and the only way to change our actions is to change our thinking first. Why would kids be any different? In fact, if we can teach them early on to become more aware of their thoughts, maybe we can save them from some harmful life decisions down the road.

So instead of jumping at the chance to punish misbehavior, can we challenge ourselves to step back, listen, and think for a moment? Instead of shutting them down as quickly as we can, let's give them the chance to share their thoughts. Let's remind ourselves: "Don't react to them. First, listen to them." We might be surprised at the outcome.

Here's a story that still makes me chuckle, but

should also make us think: I was in the fourth grade at Jefferson Elementary School in Iola when I hatched a brilliant plan to get all the girls in my class to kiss me. There was a little dollar store back then on Main Street called Kresge's. One day, I walked in there and stole all the jewelry I could get my hands on. (I was really good at stealing back then.) I must've pocketed 30 or 40 little 2-cent rings and necklaces without getting caught. Next day on the playground at recess, I spread the word that the girls could get free jewelry for a little kiss. I hid around the side of the school building and lined them all up. They'd come around one at a time. I'd get my kiss, and they'd get their jewelry.

The operation was going along smoothly until the principal took her place in line. She came around the corner and said, "Where's *my* ring?" She must've heard what I'd been doing because, she marched me straight into the school office where Maxine was waiting. I was whipped and kicked out of school that day. (Back then, they whipped you!)

Looking back, I wonder what made me do that. What made me take the risk of stealing and doing something I knew would get me into big trouble at school? On one hand, you could say, *"Aw, he was just being an ornery young boy."* Actions were punished. End of story. On the other hand, you could consider the thoughts behind my actions. What was my true motive?

I wanted attention. I wanted affection, never had it much at home. Needed it so much, I'd steal to get it. Saw all of this sex and kissing happening right in front of me with my mother and countless men. Was that love? My young fourth-grade mind absorbed it all, tried to make sense of it, and eventually those thoughts turned into actions.

We cannot underestimate the effect that we as adults have on the lives of the children in our care. I learned this firsthand as a father and in the 10 years I spent teaching and coaching in the Kansas City area. For me, it was a time of investing in the lives of young people—being truly present with them, challenging them, and helping them feel cared for and understood. It was an opportunity to take what had happened to me in my own past and turn it around—to inspire and uplift these students and athletes who were entrusted to my care. Hearing from many of them, even decades later, has reminded me how crucial it is we take the time to connect with the hearts and minds of kids in every generation.

Not long ago, an 82-year-old man walked right up to me in a local restaurant. He said, "You don't remember me, but I just loved you. You taught my son at Shawnee Mission West 45 years ago. He ran Cross Country, and nobody ever came to the meets to watch them run.

"It was never one of the more popular sports," he continued. "One day in class, my son told you how discouraged he felt that no one showed up to support his team. And do you know what you did that next Saturday? You brought your whole football team out to the finish line at the Cross Country meet. I'll never forget it. He had a hundred kids cheering him on. Meant the world to him."

"I'm sorry sir, I don't remember it," I said. That was 40-some years ago.

And he said, "*I* remember it. You made an impact on me as a young father and inspired us as a family. We still talk about it to this day. Thank you, Coach Rodrock."

I have so many stories like this one, and I'm honored to know that all these years later there are still families benefitting from the connections we made so many years ago.

The wife of a former wrestler called me awhile back. She said, "We're having a surprise 50th birthday party for my husband, *and you're going to be there.*"

I said, "Well that's real sweet of you, honey, but this is a busy month for me..."

"Oh, no, no, no," she said. "This family was raised with Coach Rodrock stories. You're going to be at his birthday party."

"Well, I'll have to see if it works with my schedule..." I said.

And she answered, "Oh, it'll work out, Coach. *You're going to set the date.*"

What could I say to that?

You see, the impact I was able to have on her husband's life has carried through all these years. He was a young man headed for some serious trouble in high school, and for some reason we had a connection, at just the right time.

I was his teacher and wrestling coach his sophomore year in 1976. The school had a tornado warning one afternoon, and we all went to the basement. Sirens, strong winds, lightening—it was bad. So we're all hunkered down, and what does this kid do? Walks by the fire alarm and sets it off. All hell breaks loose. The ambulance comes, police, and fire engines come, and of course we all have to go outside! It's a torrential downpour. More than 2,000 students, principals, teachers, counselors...we're all sopping wet.

Well, eventually the storm passed, but this guy was in hot water and was about to be kicked out of school. So I loaded him up and drove him to the reform school in Topeka, Kan. I wanted him to see just where his life was headed. A friend of mine who worked there gave us a good tour. It was not a pretty sight. "This is where you're going," I told the kid as he looked around at others who'd ended up in that place. That little trip totally changed his life.

I left my coaching job not long after, but that boy never forgot me. He was a two-time state wrestling champ and told me once, "Every time I wrestled, you were in my heart, Coach Rodrock."

Well, needless to say, I showed up at his surprise party. And our friendship continues to this day.

I don't believe I had the magic touch when it came to coaching, but I had the desire to invest in those young lives, to help them build character, strength, and self-confidence. Letting a young kid know that they matter through your words and actions—that's something they don't ever forget.

The kids I coached always knew I believed in them 100%, but more importantly, I taught them to believe in *themselves*. I knew that's what would carry them beyond school, beyond coaches, and through the rest of their lives. I always looked for ways to help them discover their own greatness, but in my 11 years as a coach, I never talked about winning. I never expected my students to be the best at everything, because I knew they couldn't be. None of us can be. We all have our own gifts, and we are just naturally better at some things than others. But that doesn't mean we can't try our hardest and have the satisfaction of knowing we gave it everything we had. I know I can't jump as high as Michael Jordan or run as fast as an Olympic world champion, but I can be the best that *I* can be. I may not be the best developer in the world, but I'm the best that Darol Rodrock can be. When I've done what I can do with the gifts I've been given, I feel a great sense of accomplishment.

I counsel coaches and teachers to inspire every one of their kids to be the very best person he or she can be—character, discipline, attitude, hard work, overcoming adversity, thinking on their feet. Let them know there's purpose in the race—not just in the win. Our wrestling team won multiple state championships, but our focus was never winning, on the outcome of the match. A match is over in a few minutes, a school year is over in a few months...but the character you build will last a lifetime.

In the end, I believe it's all about taking the time to connect with kids. Listen to their hearts—not just their words. Always inspire them to believe in themselves, and remind them often that every decision, no matter how small it may seem today, matters in the end.

"A Man Never Stands So Tall As When He Stoops To Help A Child. "
This is one of Darol's favorite beliefs.

Darol hugging one of the children at the
Darol Rodrock Foundation Holiday Party.

17

THE HISTORY OF YOU

A book you're writing every day

It's not only children who need to be reminded that their choices can make a powerful difference. We all leave a legacy through our daily lives.

I taught American History at Shawnee Mission West High School. I'm fascinated by history, and while I wanted to help my students learn all about the subject, there was something even more important I wanted them to learn about—themselves. After all, those who aren't aware of history are doomed to repeat it, right? This applies even more to those desperately trying to escape the shadows of their past.

I told my students that there are all kinds of history books in the world—Civil War history, Kansas history, American history...the list goes on. But there's another kind of history book that's far more important for each one of us, and that's the personal history we are writing with our own lives. Day by day, we add pages to our books.

I sometimes ask people "Could I read what you've written in your history book? Would you be proud of every one of your pages?" I can tell you I wouldn't want you to read every single page of my history book. I've done my best, but we all have things we wish we hadn't written there. It's so important to fill our books with pages of which we're proud. I always told my students, "Don't do something in your life that you wouldn't want to see in your history book or that you wouldn't want someone else to read. Think hard about a choice before you make it." Being arrested, taking drugs, having an unplanned pregnancy—these are all choices we can't undo... things that can change the course of our lives forever. And you only get one life—one chance to write this book.

Now, if we want to ensure our stories are written well, we need a vision for our lives. In fact, I liken it to going on a trip. If I told you I was taking you on a vacation, what's the first question you'd ask me? *"Where are we going?"* If I said we were going skiing, you'd want to take winter clothes. If I told you we were going to South America, you'd want to take a swimsuit. Hunting, fishing, boating...wherever your trip is taking you, you'd want to pack your suitcase according to your destination, wouldn't you? I pack my suitcase in my life with the things I need in order to get where I want to go. Before I live each day, buy a piece of ground, do anything...I know where I'm going. I know what I want to accomplish and what it's going to take to get there. We are all on a trip. Where are we going? Where are our lives leading? What do we want out of this journey? What do we need in our suitcases for a successful trip?

When I quit teaching, I knew I wanted two things: To never be poor again and to have the freedom to use my time as I wished. So I had to pack my suitcase accordingly.

Ask yourself: What do I want for my life? My family? My kids? Think about it, and talk about it with your partner, if you have one. Make sure your history book is written the way you want it be!

But be careful: Many people never get past the physical part of living. They don't slow down to nurture their spirits. They want a bigger house, more money, more cars, boats...the list goes on. Instead of being intentional about the truly important, lasting things in life, they use all their energy trying to acquire more and better things. They don't consider the destination of their hearts, and they come up empty in the end.

We're all faced with choices to make every day, and sometimes it's the little ones that add up to make the biggest difference. We have to be intentional about where our lives are going or those choices may lead us down the wrong path; our history books will not have the ending we want.

Here's one (slightly humorous) way I learned this lesson: Picture a rainy, chilly night in the springtime, back in 1962. I'd invited my high-school sweetheart to join me to pick up night crawlers in the park. (I was a big fisherman in high school.) We picked up a bucket-load, I think, and put them in the trunk. We were soaked, and we snuggled in the car for a while, and I caught a terrible cold.

That weekend happened to be the high-school state-champion track meet—something I'd been training so hard for. My event started, and I easily moved ahead of everyone—60 or 70 yards—running the best race of my life. I had about 200 yards left to go. Suddenly, the cold I'd caught a few days before while picking up night crawlers hit me in a big way. I felt like I had just picked up a piano and was carrying it on my back. I got beat in a dead heat by another kid. I was so disgusted with myself. But what could I do?

It's a permanent page in my history book.

Other decisions can have much greater consequences, changing the course of our lives forever. Recently, one of our homebuilders was out walking in rural Missouri. A car went flying by recklessly, so he yelled at the driver to slow down. The car stopped, the men got into an altercation, and the homebuilder knocked him down. The driver drove off, found something to use as a weapon, and came back and killed the homebuilder. Going to spend the rest of his life behind bars because of a choice he made in anger.

And as devastating as some choices turn out to be, we have to remember *it's not the last page in our history book until we take our final breath.* I know folks in prison, friends who've lost everything, others whose lives have been ravaged by addiction. I try to remind them that if we're still breathing, there are more pages to be written. No matter what circumstances we find ourselves in, we can choose what to write today.

However, if we get stuck in a past mistake—frustrated by something we wish we hadn't done and now we can't undo—it can cast a huge shadow in our lives. Instead of moving forward and making a new start, we may get caught in a "would've, could've, should've" mindset, feeling hopeless, paralyzed today by something we did yesterday. *But we always have a choice to step back into the light again!* If we can learn from our experiences and give ourselves grace instead of judgment, I call that "wisdom." However, if we keep making the same mistakes over and over again, I call that *having experiences that we just don't learn from.* You just have one experience after another until you finally learn, *I don't want to do that anymore.*

Most importantly, our history books are not about reaching perfection. They are about learning from the past, gaining wisdom for the future, and filling our pages with all the good we can in the time we are given. Remember, it's your story. No one else can write it. What a fun and exciting challenge in our lives. What will you add to your book today? Remember: Only you can write this page.

Dr. Thomas presenting Darol his diploma at his graduation in 1962.

Darol running track his senior year in Marysville.
He placed 2nd in State with a time of 1:58 for the half mile.

18

I CAN & I WILL

Once you believe it, anything is possible

There's one thing I believe is *vital* for every person who desires to live a successful life. It's a belief I hold tightly that has given me the strength to survive—and even thrive—through all of life's ups and downs.

One simple saying: ***I can and I will.***

Those who know me best would say this truth has come to define me, and I try to share it with everyone I meet.

I've heard a lot of people say, *"I can."* Many of us believe that we *can*. But what makes all the difference is believing we *will*. We *will* reach that goal. We *will* overcome that challenge. We *will* do what we set out to do.

There have been times in my own life when I wasn't sure if I was going to make it. It's almost like I was on my belly. Ever had that feeling? Maybe it's drugs, alcohol, divorce, losing a child, health problems, or unemployment. It's like you're on your belly and just can't get up.

It takes a tremendous amount of strength to push yourself up to your knees. But you've got to get there, no matter what. Then, slowly but surely, you get up on your feet and just start putting one foot in front of the other—one moment at a time. And if you fall again, then get back up again! Don't let that familiar shame, anger, and frustration keep you down another moment.

People can help you, and friends can encourage you, but only YOU can choose to get back up again. This is why, if you're looking for a motivational speech, I won't give you one. But I *will* do my best to inspire you. See, I believe there's a huge difference between motivation and inspiration: Great teachers, coaches, and leaders are the ones who inspire people. When I try to motivate you, you'll eventually forget what I said. But when I *inspire* you, it changes you...it changes your spirit.

So here's my speech:

When you get up in the morning, put your feet on the floor, get your ass out of bed, and be proud of yourself. Don't wait for me or anyone else to say, "I'm proud of you." You be proud of you. You change your spirit. Thank God for this day and choose to live it in His glory. And believe from this day forward that you can and you will!

End of speech.

That's what I have to do every day, and believe me, some days I sure don't feel like it! Somehow I learned early on that to be successful in whatever I endeavored, I had to make the decision for myself. No one could make me run faster or jump higher or study harder. If I wanted to accomplish those things, I had to *choose* to follow through.

And if I chose not to, I couldn't say it was my teacher's fault, or my girlfriend's fault, or my parents' fault. If I'm going to be successful *I have to look within myself.*

In fact, I've always found these words of Jesus to be powerful and true: "Ask and it will be given to you; seek and you will find; knock and the door will be opened." [Matthew 7:7]

We've all wished for something in our lives at one time or another. Maybe it's a real need, like food or a safe place to sleep at night. Or simply something we want, enough money for a relaxing vacation or more love and happiness in our families. So many people are hoping and searching for something, but they give up before they find it. Or they don't even know how to begin looking. Where should they go? What should they do? They get frustrated and overwhelmed and can't seem to get the help they need.

It's really a lot simpler than we realize. If you're looking for land or cars or horses or money or houses—whatever it is—you need to gather all the resources you can. Stop and think about who could help you, make a plan—and then do something about it!

All my life, I've seen people who sit around waiting for something to happen magically instead of taking steps to work it out themselves. Frustrated when things don't go their way, they wonder why in the world they can't catch a break.

But I've also seen people who just seem to be *lucky* in life. They are the ones who don't wait for what they're hoping for. They know how to ask and seek and knock. They work hard and go after it!

This is why I firmly believe: **Luck is where preparation meets opportunity.** I've always said that a lot of people may be smarter than me, *but they won't get any luckier than I am.*

First of all, I always have a plan. I am constantly working to create environments where I can be lucky.

I know if I prepare for the opportunity—prepare harder than the smarter guy—then when the moment comes to win the match, pass the test, find the job, get the sale—I've prepared for it more than anyone else.

About 25 years ago, I found a way to remind myself of this daily: a personalized license tag on my truck that says *LDR*. It stands for *Lucky Darol Rodrock,* which has been my nickname for years.

I earned the name early on as a wrestling coach. It seemed like we were always losing matches at the very end, so I created a drill for my wrestlers that prepared them to do whatever they needed to win in those last few seconds. Soon we were winning match after match!

I'll never forget the wrestling state championship in 1974. My heavyweight, Mark, was behind 3-2, flat on the mat, looked like a sure defeat. The crowd was going crazy. "Come up, Mark...COME UP!" we'd all begun shouting. With two seconds left, he just lifted his head, picked that guy up, turned him over on his back, and won the match at the buzzer. The place went wild.

Now someone watching that match might say, "Wow, that guy got lucky!" But the truth is, we had prepared for that very opportunity. We'd built our strength and endurance all year long, and no one was in better shape than we were. We'd have those boys work out by carrying cinder blocks. We would do the wheelbarrow during practice, hold their legs in the air, and make them walk on their hands 100 yards. They just wore themselves out, but they absolutely refused to give up.

So people would say to me, "You lucky sucker! How do your boys keep winnin' those matches?"

Of course, I'd just smile and answer, "Guess it's just luck! That's all I can say..."

Then I quit teaching and went into real estate, and the same kind of thing happened. I knew to buy the best location: close to schools, close to grocery stores, close to churches, close to everything. I did my research, studied the market, knew my business, and did everything I could ahead of time to give myself the advantage. So I'd buy the best location and turn around and sell more lots than anyone. And early on in my real-estate career, I'd make money on every piece of ground I bought. "You lucky sucker," people would say, "you seem to make money on everything."

Here's a childhood story I like to share to illustrate my point: My foster dad, Ray, planted corn one year, and guess what? It didn't rain. He lost his whole corn crop.

The next year he planted corn again, and it didn't rain. Lost his corn crop again. Everybody did. And they lost everything.

The third year when Ray planted corn I said, "Dad, *why are you planting corn*? You lost money two years in a row!"

He looked at me and said, "But I think it's gonna rain this year, Darol."

And it did! And nobody else had corn, because they'd given up too soon. But we had a bumper crop, and the price was high! So the moral of the story is: *If you don't plant your corn, you can't get lucky.*

It's true for everything in life. If you don't prepare and study, you won't get your degree. If you don't get ready for the interview, you won't get the job. I don't care what it is you're looking for, if you're not willing to work harder than the next guy and prepare for the opportunity, then don't expect luck to follow you around.

Obviously, I don't always receive everything I ask, seek, knock, and pray for—I'm not always the "lucky one"—but I'm always moving ahead with the belief that good things will happen if I keep sowing those seeds. And even if it's not exactly what I'm hoping for, I'll find something close enough so that I'm happy and satisfied and grateful.

Regardless, if you have a dream, *don't be afraid to give it a try*. With your belief in yourself and the power God has given you to make great things happen, you never know where "I can and I will" might take you!

"Lucky Darol Rodrock".

19

TRUE FRIENDSHIP

The spiritual gift that lasts a lifetime

For those of us who come from pasts filled with abuse and isolation, it can be very difficult to develop trusting relationships later in life. But the respect my friends have shown me has given me a much greater sense of self-worth. Friendship has truly been a light in my darkness—a vital part of my healing and ongoing support system—and I believe there's much more to it than we often realize.

My friends in high school and college had a far bigger impact on me than many of them probably knew. They validated me, built me up, and grew my self-esteem in ways Maxine and Whitford never could or did. Can you imagine how it felt to be elected class president by my friends in Marysville? This was huge for me.

My fraternity brothers set an example I had to work hard to match. They set the bar high in the grades they earned and in the way they acted. I know I would have never made it through KU without their influence. If I had ended up at a less intellectual fraternity, would I have been driven to work as hard? I don't think so. I owe those young men so much. In fact, Proverbs 13:20 says: *"Walk with the wise and become wise, for a companion of fools suffers harm."* And I think that says a lot about the power of friends.

And in low times, my friends have been an absolute means of survival. I didn't have family I could turn to when life got rough. When things got hard, when I got low, it wasn't my mom or dad who I could call to help lift my spirits. (I know this is particularly true for kids in foster care. Their friends BECOME their family!)

My friends have been a safety net to me time and time again. They've been one of the keys in helping me recognize and leave the shadows of my past behind me. This is also why choosing the right friends is so important. True friends are there to support you, build you up, hold you accountable, and show you what good living looks like. In my talks, I urge people to look for friends who fit this bill. Don't waste time on people who drag you down, set a bad example, or disappear when you need them. (The saying, "Tell me who your friends are, and I'll tell you your future" really hits the nail on the head.) A friend is a spiritual gift from God, so we need to choose wisely—and tend those relationships carefully!

We can all mention things friends have done for us throughout our lives, but one story I'll never forget is about my dear friend Kenny: Almost 40 years ago, I had a Brittany bird dog named Suzie—one of my favorites in my lifetime. I'd lost her collar somehow, so my best friend Kenny put one of his on her. It showed his name and address; he lived about 25 miles from me. Well, I was out of town one day and a terrible blizzard came up, with bitter cold and ice everywhere. Suzie got out of her pen somehow, and a neighbor found her. He called the number on the collar, which was Kenny's.

He said, "I've got your bird dog here. It must've gotten out."

Kenny said, "No, my dog's in his pen. Where do you live?"

"Gardner," said the man.

"Oh that must be Darol Rodrock's dog! He's got my collar on his dog."

The man said, "Oh, I know Darol Rodrock. I'll just

take the dog over and put her back in the pen."

Kenny said, "No, I'll drive up and do it. I want to make sure she doesn't get out again. That's Darol's favorite dog of all time. He just loves her."

So Kenny drove through that blizzard on a six-hour round-trip drive that normally would have taken about 40 minutes. He even slid off the road into the ditch at one point!

"Well, Rock," he said afterward, "I just didn't want you to lose your dog."

That's just one example. I could tell hundreds of stories about things my friends and I have done for one another. I am so grateful to be blessed with those friendships—some I've had for more than 50 years!

So what's the secret to maintaining a lifelong friendship? I can tell you what's been true for me, and just like everything else, you'll have to decide for yourself what makes sense to you.

I believe you never criticize a friend. Encourage, uplift, nurture, inspire, and love—but never criticize. Rather than pointing out what others see as "flaws," I try to focus on the positive things about my friends. I try to remind them often of the traits I appreciate about them. Maybe it's their wisdom, their passion, their loyalty—whatever it is, I know I can learn from them and hopefully incorporate those things into my life, too.

I find it interesting that many people give what they call "constructive criticism." They try to differentiate that from just plain *criticism*. I see constructive criticism as simply a case of one person believing that his or her values and opinions are what someone else ought to live by. If someone gives you constructive criticism, it's his or her judgment about how you're living. That's why I try and encourage people to inspire, love, nurture, and lift up—not criticize.

Never let your ego get in the way of a friendship. Sadly, I've seen this happen more than once in my life. People let sex, money, jealousy, competition, expectations, power, and other things get involved and they lose a friend over it. Instead of respecting friendship as a spiritual gift from God and protecting it with all they have, they choose some temporary satisfaction and throw away what could have been a lifelong blessing.

Focus on how you can help a friend, not what you can get from them. Years ago, one of my dearest friends of 40 years had a piece of ground that he was just about to lose. He couldn't make the $175,000 interest payment, and the bank was taking the land back. He'd lost everything in a recession, and he was exhausted. Just wanted to give up. But I could see that things were going to turn around soon.

"You can do this!" I told him. "Stay the course!" I helped him get back on his feet and financed him in the building business. He's sold 30 homes in the last two years and made $12,000 a house—that's almost $360,000! I loved having the opportunity to be a good friend to him, as he has always been to me. It wasn't about the money; it was about friendship.

And one final thought to share:

Go out of your way to give yourself to others. It's simple. Always look for opportunities to open your heart to friendship. Whether you just met them or you've known them for years, you'll have more friends than you could've ever imagined.

To summarize, these are the things I try to abide by in my friendships:

Never criticize a friend.

Never let your ego get in the way of a friendship.

Focus on how you can help a friend, not what you can get from them.

Go out of your way to give yourself to others.

Sure, I've messed up and forgotten these things from time to time. I have an ego. I'm human, and I've made lots of mistakes. But first and foremost, I will always cherish a friend.

I had a 70th birthday party in 2014 to launch my foundation for foster children. I was overwhelmed by the friends and family who came to support me.

There were 2,260 in attendance, and I jokingly said, *"This wasn't much of a turnout. I thought I had more friends than that!"*

Some were new friends. Some were friends who've been with me all my life. There were friends from 13 states there. Almost half of my football team from 1962 showed up! There were folks with all different kinds of jobs, abilities, and backgrounds. Doesn't make a difference to me how much money my friends have or how successful the world believes they are. I just care about *who* they are. Regardless of how we met or how often we see each other, my friends are some of the greatest gifts in my life.

Photo taken in 2017, showing the incredible spiritual gift of friendship. These longtime friends have supported Darol throughout the years. Kenny New (since 1972), Darol, Larry O'Donnell (since 1974), Jerry Mullin (since 1967), Jerry Reilly (since 1982).

Darol, Bill Grigsby, and Bob Craft, both friends of 35 years.

20

TURN THE FUNNEL
UPSIDE DOWN

Which end are you looking through?

Friendship is just one part of my life that has expanded beyond what I ever imagined it could. Through the years, I've learned what can happen when we let go of limitations in every area of our lives.

Let me explain: Each day I choose to look at life through a funnel. (People kind of chuckle when I tell them that, but it's true!) It's one way I believe we can live with more and more light and less shadow every day.

Did you ever look through a funnel from the top down? As you look into the funnel from the big end, the shaft gets very narrow. There's not much light down there, is there? It gets smaller and smaller, kind of like going through a tunnel. But if you turn that funnel upside down and look through the little end, you can see that it gets bigger at the top—unlimited expansion!

I think the following illustration explains my point: When we put oil in a car, we pour it into a funnel that's wide at the top but gets narrower as it flows down into the car. At some point it occurred to me that life's kind of like that. We start out young, opportunistic, idealistic. We're excited about living. Maybe we go to college, get married, have families. We're ready to take on the world.

As we get older, our lives move into the shaft of the funnel. Things start to narrow. We may get stuck. We age. Maybe people lose their jobs, have health problems, become disillusioned by politics, get a divorce, don't feel good most days...whatever the case may be. Our world starts to shrink down; we cease to be expansive in our thinking. Matter of fact, we may become downright cynical. We no longer wake up feeling refreshed and resourceful, ready for whatever the day may bring.

I've noticed it happens especially with the older

people in my life. That's why I try to encourage them—and people of all ages—to avoid getting caught in the shaft. If we will expand our consciousness by turning the funnel upside down, then each day can bring new and exciting thoughts and discoveries—*not* narrow-minded fear and complaining. In fact, I've realized that as I age I have all kinds of opportunities if I just look for them. I believe everyone has something to offer to others, up and until their last day on Earth.

Whether we're 80 or 50 or 30 or 10, this day holds the same 24 hours of opportunity. As long as we don't get caught up in being cynical, sarcastic, mean-spirited, or self-centered in our lives, there will always be a tremendous opportunity to see possibilities in the world. We can all live abundant lives of service, helping the world to be better than the way we found it. But the chance to enrich each other's lives will only come if we don't get caught in the shaft of the funnel. We can't bring light to others if we can't see it ourselves.

A friend of mine called recently, feeling completely discouraged about finding a job. He said, "Darol, I've been turned down 30 times."

I said, "Well, maybe you haven't tried hard enough."

He answered, "I just don't think I have it in me."

"Then go find a different kind of job," I told him. "Maybe this isn't the right opportunity for you."

"But it's where I want to be!" he insisted.

"Well, then go again, and don't measure how many times you've been turned down. Enjoy the process of going. Just keep going, and *don't give up.*"

I encouraged him to change his focus from the impossibilities to all the possibilities. He was looking from the top of the funnel down that day, but he really needed to turn it upside down and look from the bottom up.

And he's not alone. There is very little expansive thinking in most people's lives today. Seems the more formal education and religion we get, the more limited we become in our thinking. We tend to be influenced by the structure of what others have taught us, and we stop allowing our own thinking to expand.

Often, people will tell me, "You really help us think outside the box."

And I jokingly say, "W*hat box?* Wait a minute, wait a minute...are you putting me inside your box? I didn't know there *was* one!"

It always makes them laugh. But when you think about it, *who ever said there had to be a limit to the way we use our minds*? Who said there had to be a box? When there's a box, you close the top, and you can't see out. You live in the dark.

I often tell parents of young children "Don't teach your kids to color in the lines. And when they draw something, don't ever ask them, 'What is that?' You see, kids see it perfectly! Instead, say, *'Tell me about it, honey. Tell me what you see!'* Don't deny them their creativity."

And when I talk to people about the things of the spirit, I like to challenge them to open their hearts and minds to all the possibilities. Think about Heaven for a moment. We can't put what is eternal into a box. One definition of Heaven is "expansion." How can you be in a box and continue to expand?

I've known some wonderful people in my life who have a strong belief in God, but it seems that many of them limit the possibility of what they can believe *about* God, because of what they've been taught by their particular religion. I see this as living in a shadow of sorts.

Who knows what we haven't yet discovered? We've enlarged our understanding of so many things—medicine, health, transportation, science— but we still have such limited perspectives about eternal things like love, and kindness, and God.

The more I learn, the more I realize how little I know. I remember reading something years ago that said, if you think you've read a lot of books, walk into a library and look around. And by the way, that's just one of the hundreds of thousands of libraries in the world! With every book I read, I realize there's another hundred written about that subject that I haven't even heard of! And there are countless books about subjects I've never even read about.

Looking up into that funnel is the way I keep learning and growing every day. I want to discover more about the things I'm interested in without being threatened by anyone else's thoughts or words or beliefs about them. The universe is always expanding. Every day brings new discoveries in health, medicine, and communication. We can challenge ourselves to consider things we haven't even thought about, and maybe today we'll make a new discovery about ourselves, those around us, and our world!

That's how I want to see life—as infinite expansion, ever-growing illumination, and unlimited ability to help myself grow and understand more, and I hope to inspire others to do the same. That's something we can all do until our last day on this earth. Who knows what we might discover together?

Darol dressed the way he is most comfortable—in his signature cowboy hat.

OUT OF THE SHADOW

§

I can't end this book without sharing the most significant part of my healing and growth: my spiritual journey. I believe my life would look very different today without the foundation I was given to stand on as a young child. My personal experience with Jesus Christ became my mental, emotional, and spiritual survival. His words and actions recorded in the Bible drew me out of the shadows, illuminated my daily path, and taught me how to treat myself and others with love and compassion. I realize that every person has his or her own understanding of spirituality, and even as I share my own, I honor and celebrate your unique journey as well. I only hope that whatever my words mean to you, they will be somehow life-giving and uplifting. I offer them humbly; take them for what you will.

§

OUT OF THE SHADOW

21

FINDING MY WAY TO JESUS

Discovering life's meaning in His words

All that I've shared with you truly comes from the gift I received in that orphanage more than 60 years ago—the real, saving love of Jesus Christ. Jesus became my friend and has walked with me ever since.

In that place, I took the first step out of the shadows of my past and into the glorious light of hope and freedom. It certainly didn't happen all at once, but little by little over time, I've learned to let go of the pain and live with more love, peace, and goodness each day.

This is simply my *way* of life—more than a philosophy or a perspective, it's part of the very fiber of my being. It encompasses all my sayings, my choices, my character, and my relationships— everything that makes me who I am.

It all started when Miss Pinnt told me about this guy named Jesus. He became a very close, personal friend of mine who helped me in life—who saw me through many days and nights of abuse, neglect, and loneliness. My relationship with Him was never about attaining some sort of holiness or getting into Heaven someday. It was about survival. And all through the ups and downs of my life, He has continued to be there...more real to me than I can possibly explain.

I didn't discover all my beliefs in one place. Never found a church where I sat down, got all the answers and thought, *Finally! Now this is what I believe! This is where I belong!* Rather, through the years, I've had experiences with many different denominations— Lutheran, Methodist, Presbyterian.

For years, I'd be in church looking up at the minister and wondering: *How could there be just one sermon for everyone on Sunday? Is that sermon supposed to fit all of us sitting here listening?* It wasn't that I disagreed with what they were saying. Instead, the message just didn't serve as power in my life, because it didn't come from my own interpretation of God's word.

Living by someone else's words and ideas has just never worked for Darol Rodrock. I guess I've always been too independent. (I had to be to survive!) I knew I needed to make sense out of the words of Jesus in my own way. Again, it doesn't mean I believe that my way is right for anybody else. But for me, personally, challenging myself to understand His words in a way that made sense in my own mind and heart have made me a stronger person. I needed to encourage myself—in essence you might say *preach* to myself—the words of Jesus every day.

I learned along the way to not just accept what others told me (that I was worthless, no good, or unworthy of being loved). I had to form my own thoughts and choose to believe that I was worth something. As I grew older, I continued to challenge others' thoughts and beliefs. I didn't just buy everything others tried to teach me.

I remember thinking at some point: *Wait, all the things these denominations are teaching—they were decided by a group of men. Why aren't women allowed to think and be part of interpreting the Bible? And if those 12 men who walked with Jesus could understand the word of God in their own way, why can't I do the same?* Even among those men there were disagreements! I wanted to know: Did it take education to interpret the Word of God or did it take wisdom? Or both? So I studied, and I learned, and I prayed for wisdom to help me interpret Jesus' words so they could benefit me every day of my life.

I have always been full of questions; I guess that's my nature. I think that questioning other people's thoughts and words as well as my own helps expand my mind and my spirit. There are so many perspectives in the universe. Just because I believe or you believe something doesn't make it right. That's very hard for some of us to accept. But I do think our personal beliefs are what form us; they're what make a difference in our lives.

None of what I'm about to share is for preaching *to* you or *at* you or telling you how anyone should live. That's a decision each of us has to make for ourselves. You see, my beliefs are pretty simple. It's based on my lifelong relationship with the words of Jesus: How I incorporate them into my daily life and how I find meaning and hope in His words. I found that if I don't use the Bible, the Bible has no use. For me, the messages of Jesus helped lead me out of the darkness of my past and into the promising light of my future.

22

BORN AGAIN

What it means to me to be saved

There's one biblical story that has helped to shape my life and bring light to my understanding of Jesus more than any other. It has become the lens through which I see all the other teachings in the Bible. It begins when Jesus meets Nicodemus in the garden one night [John 3:1-21].

Nicodemus is an older man and one of the church leaders; Jesus is a young man educated in the Jewish religion. Jesus has grown up with a deep understanding of the history and tradition of His people. But now He's teaching a new version of the law—a new love and a new acceptance that is summed up by one Commandment: *Love your neighbor as yourself.* He also teaches us: *The Kingdom of God is within you. The Kingdom of God is here.* These thoughts are mentioned numerous times in the New Testament.

As they walk and talk together in the garden that night, Jesus looks at Nicodemus and says, "You must be born again."

I imagine Nicodemus chuckling and saying, *Jesus, I'm an old man. How can I be born again?*

And Jesus answers in essence, *I don't mean of the body, Nicodemus. I mean of the spirit.* There is a spiritual life within each of us, and we must all be born into that spirit in hopes of seeing and entering the Kingdom of God.

That conversation is what influenced my thinking about the true message Jesus came to share. The foundation of all my beliefs came from this young, 30-year-old man saying to this older man that *you must be born in the spirit to enter the Kingdom of God.*

I believe that Bible verse gave me a deeper understanding of all the words Jesus spoke. I discovered that his words are above the ego, the body, the world—they reveal a divine realm. They're like the wind. He says we don't know where the wind comes from or where it goes, but it's there.

So what does it mean to be born again, in the

spirit? Or as some people say, to be "saved?" It's a question we all have to answer for ourselves. Does it mean I'm going to Heaven? Does it mean I believe in Jesus Christ? That I believe in God? That I live a different life than others? I can tell you that for me, it means something special every day. It means I want to live in the light—be born in the spirit and saved *every day.*

If it's just about getting into Heaven someday, then what good is it today? I need light for *today.* I need peace and love and acceptance *in this moment.* I need a way to make it through each day—to be aware that I can accept and live a life in the grace of God. When I find myself getting angry, wanting to judge, or maybe the shadow of my ego starts to take over, I need to feel Jesus' love. The more I feel it, the more I can relax into the quiet, peace, and grace that He's given me. I feel safe knowing Jesus will be there for me in any moment, no matter what kind of rejection or loneliness I may experience. To me, that's what it is to be born again, moment by moment, day by day.

It's a choice we all get to make each day. Will we live this day being saved in the name of Jesus Christ? Or won't we? Will we be angry and bitter, mean and stressed, or worried, hateful, and murmuring? Or will we choose love and grace, peace, kindness, generosity, and gratitude—living as much like Jesus as we can?

And we can live in oneness with Him.

When I look back someday, I want to see a life lived in that light of God's grace, not in darkness of the shadow. I want to know I've done everything I could with this one life I've been given. It's the greatest gift we'll ever receive—the gift of being born. And with that gift comes the gift of dying.

The question is then: What are you going to do with each day in between those two gifts? We have a choice of what we do with our actions and our thoughts every day of our lives between birth and death. I make every effort to choose to live in the grace and love of God. Knowing there's an end to this life encourages me to live every day like it's my last.

And when that day comes, I don't want look back and realize I took my life for granted. Sure, I've let my ego take over and missed some wonderful opportunities. I don't want to waste any more time living in the ego. I want to live in the spirit—in the peace and quiet of God's grace.

I don't know where Heaven is or what happens when we get there. That doesn't concern me much. By living *today* in His grace, I don't worry about tomorrow.

Nicodemus' story confirms to me that Jesus' message is about the spirit. He's telling us that we can be born again in the spirit and rejoice each day, no matter what our circumstances are. And I repeat: *No matter what circumstances we face.*

OUT OF THE SHADOW

23

THE KINGDOM OF GOD

*Finding the Kingdom today,
not in some distant place*

To say a message is about the spirit doesn't mean it's about ignoring our bodies. God has given us these wonderful vessels to house our spirits, to experience the world around us, and to connect with the people who share our lives. To be fully present in the moment, mind, body, and spirit—that's what living in the Kingdom of God is to me. Here's how I've come to understand this beautiful reality.

Going through so much as a child, mentally and

physically, made it very difficult to find peace in my life. Especially in my teenage years, I'd find myself overreacting to things—getting upset easily or just being angry all the time. I'd take things personally, feel rejected, isolated, fall into the trap of becoming a "victim." I was reacting to the past, and it was stealing my joy in the present.

Miss Pinnt had told me about something called the Kingdom of God long ago at the orphanage, and through the years I found myself wondering if this "kingdom" was even real. What was it? Where was it? And who lived there? I wanted to know what Jesus said about it, so I started researching in the Bible. It didn't happen all at once, but I slowly came to the conclusion that the Kingdom of God is here, now, not in a distant time or place. When I speak of coming out of the shadows, this is the light I'm talking about.

These days, when people ask me how I am, I like to tell them, "If I was any better, I'd think I was in Heaven." And then I say, "Hey! Maybe we are!"

My answer usually catches them off guard. Some look at me funny. Others say, "Welllll, I'm not sure about that..."

I understand their hesitation. You see, for so long I understood that we're "waiting" to live in God's light. I learned that we have to die to go to Heaven; we can't enjoy it today. But for me, Heaven is now. My spirit can radiate peace and love and joy in this moment. Jesus said the Kingdom of God is today. Not yesterday, not tomorrow...not some day in the distant future, or some other place we haven't reached.

I don't try to tell people what to believe, but I know what I believe: the Kingdom of God is a spiritual reality that exists within each of us—if we will just seek it.

Can you imagine Jesus, a young man standing on the synagogue steps? He's preaching to a mass of people as He often did, and suddenly the Scribes and the Pharisees walk out of the temple door with these big long robes and beards, with books of the Jewish law in their hands. They ask Him: *Where is this Kingdom you speak of?*

And He looks back up at them and says: *Don't look up or look down—for the Kingdom of God is within you!* That Bible verse, Luke 17:21, truly changed my life.

My friends, these are the people who condemned Jesus, and He *still* saw the Kingdom of God in them. But His claim about the Kingdom threatened those religious men—made them furious.

We're the church! The Scribes insisted. *We've got the Kingdom here in our walls, inside our tabernacle! We don't know what this Kingdom is You're talking about.*

Imagine Jesus saying: *Don't wait to celebrate your*

*life. I found the spirit and divinity in Me, the peace in Me, the love in Me, the connection with God. And I'm telling you that it's all within you, too! Give up the world. Give up your ego, your fear, your anger—give it all up. Accept that the Kingdom of God is in you and is **real**—a real experience of peace, love, and joy.*

In the Lord's Prayer, Jesus proclaims: "Our Father, Who art in Heaven, hallowed be Thy Name." And then He says: "Thy Kingdom come, Thy will be done, *on Earth as it is in Heaven.*"

I believe He was telling His Father: I hope they understand as I pray to You, that You want Your Kingdom to come—that You want everything done on Earth **now** as it is in Heaven.

That's the message I receive whenever I hear that powerful prayer. He says it so many times in the New Testament: *The Kingdom of God is here; the Kingdom of God is in you; the Kingdom of God is nigh.* I believe that's the main message of Jesus. *Darol*, He tells me. *Open your eyes. Don't be blind. Don't be dead. See my Kingdom here, now, in this very moment, in every person you meet.* You *can be saved, Darol, because the Kingdom of God is here!*

But what about the man who murders? Can he have the Kingdom in him? And the woman consumed with anger? And the prostitute... stoned, condemned, and filled with shame. Can they have the Kingdom of

God in them?

Oh yes, it's there, no matter who we are or what we've been through. Sometimes the Kingdom gets covered up and darkened by our egos or the shadows of our past. Sadly, some people are just never told that the peace and love of God can exist in them.

I always try to choose kindness toward people, not because I want to get something out of it, but because I see God's image in them. I may get run over because people don't see the Kingdom of God in *me*, but I see it in them.

We need our connections with one another. Little children understand this innately; they see each other so much more clearly than we do. They haven't yet allowed their egos to lead them into judgment like many adults have. Until they're shown otherwise, children aren't preoccupied with who has more money or who looks different. They're just celebrating life together, living in the moment, and loving each other in their own simple way. When we understand that every human being has Christ inside of them, we are able to see people differently too—with love and not with judgment.

Another way I've found to live in the Kingdom of God each day is to choose an attitude of gratitude, moment by moment. For me, the most important moment in life is the one we're living right now. It's not a moment we're waiting for or a moment that happened in the past. It's this one. This breath. This heartbeat. This conversation we're sharing. It's really all we have.

So many people live in a constant hurry...their minds scattered, their attention torn between five things instead of focusing on one. They aren't able to be present here, now. And they miss some wonderful things along the way. I do it, too. I have to remind myself daily to be aware of each precious moment.

Since we live in a world like this—a busy, distracted, hurry-up world—how can we bring ourselves back to the moment, no matter what our circumstances are? How can we be fully present, enjoying the company of each person we encounter— even enjoying the company of ourselves?

This is a very big task for me. To enjoy being alone is difficult, so I try to pay attention to my feelings when I'm alone. Say I'm fishing—am I savoring the moment? Or am I frustrated and missing other people? Probably comes from my childhood being alone and lonely. When there's not someone there to nurture me, I get anxious. But as I've gotten older I've learned to just try and enjoy Darol—not to be in a hurry to do something else or be someplace else.

I've also learned that I can't fully enjoy the moment I'm given if I don't have an attitude of gratitude for that moment. I try to continually shift my focus to the goodness in life, no matter what circumstance may come my way.

That is why I try to start every day with this prayer:

Thank you God for what I have.

Not for what I want or what I need, but what I have.

It's a prayer that's helped shape my life so much it has become a part of who I am. Before my feet hit the floor in the morning, those are the words that come to my heart, reminding me what my life is about.

I know that if I'm not grateful for what I have now, I will never be satisfied. This Kingdom that God has promised will always seem to be just around the corner or just over the hill—unless I make the conscious choice to be here now—finding joy wherever I am. I'm not going to spend my one precious life always trying to run ahead, wanting something more, bigger, better, faster. I'll miss all the blessings right in front of me if I'm too busy looking ahead for the next thing.

I suppose going through such dark times in the past caused me to look for the goodness, for the light, in all my circumstances. It's how I learned to survive as a child. I could either see the dismal part of life, the anger and the fear and the hate...or I could choose to somehow see the beauty of the moment. When you come from nothing, you learn to never take the little joys in life for granted.

Even during those terrible days in Arkansas, maybe the worst time in my life, I would appreciate moments of beauty. I remember I'd catch the school bus before the sun came up. Always sat by the same girl, and she became my special friend. We'd go over the Arkansas hills in that bus, and just as we'd reach the top of a certain hill, the sun would come spilling over the horizon. It was breathtaking for me, even as an 11- or 12-year-old boy, and I never tired of it. Nature's beauty, in all its forms, was healing and nurturing to me. It still is to this day.

And then there was the daily ride to school in Garnett, Kan., along old Salty Dog Road. We'd often come upon a flock of prairie chickens, thousands of them, and I'd ask the bus driver to stop. We kids wanted to see them, marvel at them—just take it all in. Kids remember to do this so much more than adults. They haven't learned how to be in a hurry yet. They're just enjoying the journey. Even before children realize what the Kingdom of God is, they live in it naturally. I've found Jesus' words to be true: "Let the little children come to Me, and do not hinder them, for the Kingdom of Heaven belongs to such as these" [Matthew 19:14].

Sometimes I'll ask a person how they're feeling: "Is your cup half full or half empty?" I'd say about 25% of those I ask are kind of down, and they tend to answer, "Half empty." About 75% of them say confidently, "Half full!"

I like to challenge them: "Why would your cup be just half full? The Bible says, 'My cup runneth over!'" I see their eyes light up like they never thought about that before. They never realized there's a third choice that is infinitely greater than the others. That's the choice I try to make. My cup runneth over.

The Bible taught me that our cups runneth over with love, appreciation, kindness, thankfulness, sharing [Psalm 23:5]. I want my cup to run over in every part of my life. I want it to overflow with the fact that I get to take the breath of life. The gift of birth and the gift of death are part of my life, and I get to choose each day how I want to live. I want to live it with my cup running over!

By the way, some days are harder than others for me. Some days I'm dealing with health problems, maybe the city's beating me up on my business, or I have relationship troubles, or whatever. However, I quickly become aware that if I want to change my attitude, I have to start with gratitude. My greatest advice to anyone is to find a way to be thankful, no matter what life brings. Could things be better? Yes.

Could things be worse? Yes. But here's the truth about life: It is what it is. We can look at our lives, just as they are, and make the decision to live with our cups running over, no matter what.

I once asked a minister friend of mine, "Is your cup half full or half empty?"

And he said, "It's half full every day!"

I smiled and said, "I guess you didn't learn in seminary that your cup runneth over, because the Bible says my cup runneth over!"

His eyes brightened. He hadn't ever even considered that thought.

He texted me a few weeks later to say he'd begun to ask his congregation each Sunday whether their cups were half full or half empty. Then he'd remind them, "Your cups runneth over with love!"

He said, "Thank you for teaching me that every day of life can be a cup running over with appreciation and love in Jesus Christ." Not long ago I learned he quit his job at the church and went to work in the Appalachian Mountains to help foster children.

I encourage you to see your life as a cup running over, even with life's challenges and difficulties. They'll happen. That's part of your ego—part of your body. But the spirit is full of love all the time, and there's no limit to the goodness we can share.

The more opportunities we take to stop and just

appreciate what we have in this moment—be it the beauty of nature, of connectedness, of another soul— the happier and freer our hearts will be. No circumstance can ever take this away from us.

That's what I call living in the Kingdom of God.

OUT OF THE SHADOW

24

MISSING THE MARK

Sin and forgiveness

I want to be clear that I don't expect myself (or anyone!) to live in a perfect state of spiritual bliss all the time. The world we live in is filled with darkness and light, and I believe our lives reflect that reality. I think it's important to acknowledge the fact that we all fall short sometimes. Sometimes our aim is off, and we find ourselves in need of grace and encouragement to make a new start. What we *don't* need in those moments is judgment and condemnation.

For me, it was a shift in the perspective of "sin" and "forgiveness" that made all the difference: Years ago, I learned that "sinne" is an Old English word that literally means to "miss the mark." It's an archer's term, referring to the aim of an arrow at a target. When the archer shoots for the bull's-eye, they don't hit it every time. They "sinne." Somewhere along the way, the word became "sin."

So for me, "sin" simply means I missed the mark—in my thoughts, my actions, in the way I love other people. If I judge, complain, expect certain things, and become anxious, I fall out of a glory that God has given me to live in today. The sinne is against me. It's about missing the mark I set for myself by not staying in the glory, grace, love, and peace God gave me.

And when it happens, I don't have to judge or condemn myself. That's not my job, and it does no good whatsoever. If I believe God loves me and every person born into this world unconditionally, then there is no room for judgment. Sometimes I find the ego takes over our spirit, causing us to miss the mark. It happens to all of us.

And when the tables are turned, and someone does something to me, I believe it isn't my job to judge them, even if they've hurt me in some way. I may be tempted to judge them. But they've just missed the mark themselves.

Years ago, I wanted to sell some hay I had stored in a barn—about 400 bales. I ran an ad in the local paper for $1 a bale.

A man called me and said, "I'll be there Saturday."

I said, "Oh, darn, I can't be there then. I'm taking my kids to a horse show. But listen, Bob, you can count." (I didn't know the man—he just answered an ad.) "Just count the hay and send me $1 a bail. I think it's around 400 bales."

On Wednesday the next week, I got a check for around $200. I asked my helper, Jose, about how many bales he thought there were. He lifted four fingers, "About 400, Señor," he said.

I sent the check back to the man and said, "You have missed the mark by trying to cheat me out of $200. I don't need the money, and I don't need the hay, but you've sinned against *yourself* by missing the mark of honesty and integrity. You didn't cheat me, you cheated yourself."

The thing is, *we* know when we complain. W*e* know when we cheat. W*e* know when we lie. We fall out of that wonderful grace and glory of God, and we can feel it in our hearts. We don't need the judgment of anyone else to let us know we've missed the mark.

Jesus said, "He who is without sin cast the first stone." Those among us who have not sinned, those among us with perfect aim every time, can cast the first stone. I don't know about you, but I'm not in that category.

I've come to believe that *the highest order of forgiveness is non-judgment.* We can let go of forgiving others for their transgressions against us for good.

Here's the story that got me to that place: Picture this guy with a cross on His back, doubled over, trudging through narrow cobblestone streets while people spit on Him, call Him names, and mock Him. He's been beaten for 24 hours by the Romans. He's been told to deny his God, and He simply won't do it. He's been tortured with leather whips with metal tips. Thorns driven deep into His head, blood running down His face, nails in His hands and feet. Now He's hanging on that cross He carried up to Calvary. Here's Jesus of Nazareth, the most wonderful man who ever lived on the face of this earth, dying a horrifying death.

Finally, when He's just about gone He says, *Kill those Romans for me, God!*

Right?

No, no. He says, Father, forgive them...FATHER, forgive them for they know not what they do. You forgive them because I don't claim the right to do that. They've done something they don't even understand, and they've missed the mark. Father, You judge that if You want to. It's in Your hands.

Jesus didn't deny what had been done to Him. He lived it, felt it, and acknowledged the pain...but He refused to cast judgment about it. And the only way I've found I can handle the hurt from my past is to say *I want to be as much like Jesus as I can—and not judge others.*

As a young child, my brain and my body suffered, no question. This brain I have today is the same brain. This body is the same body. It happened, it was real, and it's a part of who I am. But I won't judge what someone else has done to me in this world. I won't judge it, because once I do, I start to carry it. Anger, pain, disappointment, frustration, rejection, loneliness—it overwhelms me just thinking about it all.

I made the decision that I'm not going to judge what my mother, my father, or anyone else did to me in my life. I'm going to lay it down. I'm going to live in the glory of God. I've learned to say, *Father,* You *take care of my parents and my past, what they did or didn't say or do. It is not my place to judge their lives.* In my adult life, I make every attempt to feel this way. I truly believe judging others brings crucifixion to my soul.

Jesus said, "Judge not, or you will be judged the same."

We've all had pain in life that felt like nails in our hands and our feet—the pain of being beaten, or abandoned, or rejected. *Wham! Wham! Wham!* We feel those things cut right through us.

I often meet people who are stuck in that place. They have great hurts from the past. Still living with the pain of the loneliness and rejection they experienced as children, they want to know how to move on.

I tell them: "Recognize what happened. Don't deny how you felt, or how you're feeling now. Own it, be aware of the affect it has had on you, and realize it's over. Understand that the little person inside you and the big person you are today are safe. You don't have to carry the anger, fear, pain, guilt, and judgment. It's okay to let go."

Being in judgment of someone is like carrying two 50-pound buckets full of sand around all day long. You pick up this hurt or this anger because of whatever was done to you. They trespassed against you, they beat you, they raped you, they robbed you, did whatever they did...and *you* carry the burden of anger, hurt, and pain. Gets heavy hauling that around your whole life!

It's been important for me to realize that the hurt I experienced wasn't about me—wasn't *because* of me. The people who mistreated, abused, and rejected me in my life—they had stories of their own, reasons for making the decisions they made. They were who they were at that time, and I was not the cause of their anger or actions. They chose those responses themselves. *It doesn't give them an excuse to do what they did*, but it helps me let go of the shame and anger I felt and to stop blaming the child in me like it was my fault.

When the fear and judgment come up (and believe me, it still does occasionally), I remind myself that it's not the adult me who's being beaten, isolated, and traumatized. I have sympathy for the little boy in me, and I've learned to love him. But I can stand on my own two feet now. I survived. I choose to let go of the shadow of the past and the need to judge, and I can choose to live in the light of today. I believe we *all* can.

OUT OF THE SHADOW

25

CHARACTER, INTEGRITY, & THE GOLDEN RULE

Doing the right things for the right reasons

Even if I miss the mark from time to time, I'll never give up aiming for the target! And the most practical way I've found to do that is to live by one simple rule every day.

"I don't know if you've ever heard of my rule," I like to say to people. "It's one I kind of made up: *Do unto others as you'd have them do unto you.*"

I chuckle, and they all smile and tell me, "We know that rule, and you didn't make it up!" Of course I didn't make it up, but I do make every attempt to live by it fully.

A lot of people I've known through the years say you can't live by that "golden rule" and be in business. "You need to make *money* your priority," they say, "Not a rule like that!"

I tell them, "No, as a matter of fact, I've made more money by practicing that rule than I ever believed I could in my life." Instead of the money, I put the *people* first, and I've found that everything else follows.

In my housing-development business, I always try to put myself in the shoes of a person who's buying one of our homes. What would I want if I lived in that house? What if the windows were leaking, or the door didn't fit, or the roof wasn't right? Well, I'd want someone to fix the darn things, wouldn't I? If I would want that done, then wouldn't they?

I believe it is of utmost importance to treat every person with respect and dignity and honor their presence in my life. Yes, it may cost me financially, and sometimes I wish I didn't have to deal with those things, but I always want to stay true to who I want to be and not let money make my decisions—business or otherwise. Even if the other person doesn't live by my rule, I can still believe and practice it, can't I?

Years ago we had an issue with a crack in the foundation of one of our new homes. The homeowner had paid $295,000 for that house. When he saw the crack, he wanted to back out of the sale. I told him, "It's okay, we'll fix it. Won't be any problem."

Well, I thought about it overnight and decided, I wouldn't want to buy a $300,000 house with a crack in the foundation. Wouldn't want to buy a brand new car with a scratch down the side. Why would he?

So I went back the next day, gave him his earnest money back and told him why I'd made the decision. It made an impression on him. He decided to build with me again and bought another home in one of my neighborhoods. Not only that, after I fixed the crack on the original house, he had some friends come out to look at that house, and they ended up buying it!

I truly believe that if you take care of people long term, it'll always come back to you, somehow. It's what I mean when I tell people: **You get back what you send out.** If I send out love and fairness, honesty and integrity, eventually those things will come back in my life. People will treat me the way I treat them.

And sometimes other people don't see things the way I see them, but I choose not to judge that. I mustn't ever expect the other person to live by my rules. The most important thing is to stay who *I* want to be and always treat others the way I'd want them to treat me. And if someone tries to cast a shadow in my life—takes their anger out on me, tries to hurt or take advantage of me in some way—I just go on. Sure, I have the freedom to send that darkness back into the world, but I try not to. I know that if I do, those things will come back to me sooner or later.

I've been tested on this more than any of my other little sayings. It's easy to believe in these things when life is going well. However, when life gets tough and things start turning on me, it can be tempting to just let it all go and do whatever the world does. When I do start to fall into that trap, I talk myself out of it as quickly as I can. No matter what anyone has done to me, *I still want to live what I believe.*

Many years ago, I started a fence company and hired someone I trusted to do the work. Turns out, he took advantage of me, and the company lost thousands of dollars in an already difficult economy.

A particular banker at Patron's Bank in Olathe, Kan., had given me a loan for the fence company. I went to see him when we lost the money. I remember he was real soft spoken. He leaned back in his chair and said, "Well, Darol, I think we've got some problems, don't we?"

"Yes, sir," I said, "but I think we can take care of them."

I started to reach into my pocket, and he quickly said, "Well, where's your attorney?"

I said, "I don't know what you're talking about."

He said, "Normally when there's a deficiency on a loan, an attorney will come in with their client and try to negotiate the settlement."

I said, "Oh there's no problem, and there's no attorney."

"Was it $162,843 dollars and 42 cents?" I asked as I pulled out the money. "That's the number the teller gave me."

He said, "Aren't you going to *negotiate?*"

I looked at him and smiled, "Negotiate what? I owe you the money, my friend. And I have it. If I didn't have it, I'd have to come in here to tell you I don't have it. But I do, and I won't deny you the money that I owe."

He said, "I've never had a borrower come in with a deficiency without trying to have half of it written off."

I said, "I owe you the money and in good faith I'll pay you back."

Well, that incident went around the banking circles. He happened to be the president of the Banking Association of Greater Kansas City at the time. That opportunity to show character and integrity probably helped to establish me in the banking business more than anything else I've ever done.

It wasn't about me wanting anyone to be impressed with how I handled things. It just made sense to me. Doesn't matter what situation I'm in, if I owe the money, I'm going to pay it back. If I don't have all the money right now, I'll give you what I *do* have and earn the rest to pay you later. I'll move into a trailer or live in somebody's basement—whatever I have to do to pay back what I owe. And by the way, I don't pay back a loan for the sake of the bank. I pay it back for me. Because I want to stay who I want to be.

I think of Jesus' teaching: "If a man strikes you, turn the other cheek." To me, turning the other cheek isn't about saying, *Here, hit me again!* It's about turning away from the temptation to make selfish decisions. It's refusing to live a self-centered life—the kind where you lie and cheat and steal, where you'll do whatever it takes to get what you think you deserve. I don't care if other people are out for themselves. I don't have to live that way. I don't care what someone chooses to do to me out of greed or anger or jealousy. I won't be part of that. Jesus' message to me is to turn away from that kind of life. Don't stay in it. I tell myself, *"Stay who you want to be, Darol. Turn the other cheek so you can walk away."*

When it comes to matters of character, I know I can fall off the path just like the next guy, so I had to develop rules like these to help me stay on track. But at the end of the day, there's great peace in knowing I have nothing to hide, I've been authentic and forthright with the people in my life, and I have stayed true to the person I know God created me to be.

OUT OF THE SHADOW

26

LIFE AS A DISCIPLE
Following Jesus today

In the end, nothing I'm saying will make any difference unless I'm living it out each day. I can't depend on yesterday's light to keep me out of today's shadow. I need to wake up each day with a renewed commitment to follow Jesus. That's what I call "being a disciple," and it looks different for every person.

I know this much about myself: I need more than just some stories about Jesus that help me follow His example. I need to enter into His experience—to understand His heart and the hearts of those who walked with Him.

I've always been the kind of person who looks for

the story behind every picture. When I read the words of Jesus, they may tell me what He said and did, but I try to imagine the details of what was happening at the time. What was He thinking and feeling? What were the people around Him thinking and feeling?

I think about the time Jesus fed 5,000 people with seven loaves of bread. I've often wondered as He walked into that village what was going on with those people. I imagine it was the same as a lot of villages in those days. They had been pillaged by the Romans, many of the Jewish people persecuted and killed for their beliefs. Those left were mourning, sad, devastated. I can see the picture in my mind. Word had spread that Jesus was coming to this town, and people lined the streets in anticipation. They'd heard of this man of God and wanted to get a glimpse of Him, perhaps even touch Him somehow.

So He told His disciples, *"Tell them to go to the hills, and I'll feed them with God's Word."* And they went—5,000 of them, hoping to hear a word of inspiration in a very difficult time.

I imagine Jesus had a voice that was as soft as velvet, kind and gentle when He talked to you one-on-one. But when He spoke to crowds, His voice could carry across the hills. He was small, not a big, handsome 6-foot-2, blonde, blue-eyed, white guy. He had blazing brown eyes, dark skin, and long hair.

Didn't really stand out from the other Jewish men at the time except for His connection with God. (Now you understand, this is my imagination talking!)

When the people got into the hills, He started preaching to them about hope and the Kingdom of God. He told them no matter what was going on in their lives—sickness, death, misery, foreclosures, bankruptcy...all things we go through today—there was still hope, because God loved them. The bread He fed them was the bread of hope, and guess what? There's plenty of hope left over for us to receive today.

And then I imagine He turned to His disciples and said, *I'm tired. Will you please talk to these people? Go out and touch them. Tell them how much God loves them and how much I love them.*

He turns around all of a sudden, and lo and behold, there are some of us sitting under a tree listening to the sermon. He walks up and takes each of us by our hands, looks us in the eye and says, *Darol, Mike, Bob, Kathy, Mary...*for He knows each of us...*Do you believe what I told you today? Did you hear my sermon? There's bread for all of us. There's hope left for years to come. Forever. Because we belong to God's Kingdom, it is ours to claim.*

He comes to me and says, Darol, will you do what I asked you today in my sermon?

And I say, No, I'm a little angry right now, Jesus.

And He smiles and says, My child, you can't live with anger and be my disciple.

If we want to be disciples of Jesus Christ, we can't live with the heavy weight of anger and resentment. We can only live lives filled with love, grace, and peace. Then we, too, can raise the dead—the dead in the spirit. We can allow the power of God to work through us, just as Jesus did.

One of my favorite examples of this healing work is the story of the blind man in Mark 10. I can just imagine Jesus walking along an old cobblestone street, and there's this man sitting up ahead. All of a sudden the man reaches out and grabs Jesus' cloak. Peter says, *Jesus! We're gonna be late! We're giving a talk. We can't take the time.*

Just a minute, Peter, Jesus says quietly.

He sits down beside this man and says, *You're blind, aren't you?* Puts his arm around him, and all of a sudden the man starts shaking and crying. Jesus says to him, *Why are you weeping? What's wrong?*

I don't know, says the man. I have no money; I have nothing. But I feel something from you. You must be the Savior they talk about—The Christ.

Jesus pulls him close, hugs him, and says, *There are those who can see who are blind, and there are those who are blind who can feel my love. You felt my love for you today, didn't you?*

The blind man drops to his knees.

Jesus smiles and says: *Go, and you will never be blind again. You will always feel the love of God.*

I want to be Jesus' disciple. I want to help others heal by sharing the glory of living in the Kingdom. When we truly believe His words, we are healed. The anger, bitterness, resentment, jealousy, and fear can't run our lives anymore. We are no longer overwhelmed with feelings of worthlessness or rejection. We begin to experience a true friendship with Jesus that makes us want to live in a state of love and grace.

And once we believe in the words and miracles of Jesus, it's natural to express that love and joy with other people, to share the hope that's there for them. We can handle anything that life deals us, because we are safe in the spiritual love of our God.

You see, somewhere along the line Jesus said to me, *Darol, read my words in the first person.*

For God so loved the world...?

No, no, no, no, He said: For God so loved Darol.

Each Bible verse came to me as a personal statement with Jesus looking me in the eye.

So when I pick up the Bible today, I read it like it's written for me. I find the truth there that speaks to me in this moment. It doesn't make any difference to me that the walls of Jericho fell down a long time ago. What's that got to do with getting me through today?

I follow Jesus today. He's as real to me as any of you. And I listen to His words. He can look at each one of us and see in us all the things we can't see in ourselves. He sees the gifts that we have to offer the world, and He invites us to use those gifts to help heal others. As we share that hope and peace and joy we've received in the Kingdom of God, we become His disciples. He spoke to us 2,000 years ago, and He speaks to us today. And we can allow Him to speak through us. What a powerful thought that we can be locked arm-in-arm with Jesus Christ and experience His words:

> *Very truly I tell you, whoever believes in me will do the works I have done, and they will do even greater things than these, because I am going to the Father.* [John 14:12]

> *...I am the way and the truth and the life. No one comes to the Father except through me.* [John 14:6]

27

THE EGO OR THE SPIRIT

Where are we living each day?

Every day, I believe we have a powerful choice: Will we hide in the darkness of despair, or will we take another step into the healing light of hope? Will we focus on our bodies and our circumstances—aches and pains and limitations—to determine our state of mind, *or* will we allow our minds to lead and trust that our bodies will follow?

See, I believe we all have two distinct parts: the ego and the spirit. These two parts are in constant conflict—always vying to lead us in our daily decisions.

OUT OF THE SHADOW

Ego focuses on things that are important in the world and in the body—job, money, success—earthly desires and expectations that often cause a lot of stress and frustration in our lives. But Spirit says, *I don't need to live in that judgmental, worried, stressful state. I can live freely in this moment, resting in the peaceful, loving nature that's always available to me from God.*

A few years ago, at my 50th high-school reunion, an old classmate walked up to me. "Darol, I didn't know you were going to be here," he said. "Never did like you, you SOB. I was supposed to be the fastest runner at MHS until you showed up and beat me every time I ran."

"That's funny," I told him, "I always admired you. You brought out the best in me." I hugged him. "I'm sorry I never got to express that gratitude for making me run faster."

I think my response surprised him. He sent me an email afterward to apologize.

I could've handled that differently, could've let my ego take over and reacted in anger. But I tried to understand him—the frustration he's harbored all these years. In fact, no matter what people say or do, I try to never respond without giving myself a few moments of peaceful thought first. I want to remind myself to offer the other person grace; I don't ever want to tear their spirit down. (It's hard enough for all of us to keep our spirits up each day as it is!)

The truth is, we *have* to be here—our bodies are here. We've got to deal with difficult relationships, take care of the kids, pay the bills, and sit in traffic...all of those things.

Jesus knows this. He experienced life in the body! That's why He tells us to be *in* this world but not *of* it. Sure, we will face adversity in our lives that'll threaten to steal the joy of this moment. We'll have family problems, divorce, deaths, sickness, accidents, money issues. But I have found that adversity is truly a perception. The problem is not the problem. The problem is the way we SEE the problem.

The ego sees adversity as a problem. The ego will try to discourage you, defeat you, tear you down, take away your determination, and wear out your body. But the spirit will always lift you up: *Rise above this! It's not a problem, it's just something you have to deal with.*

I once read the book *Man's Search for Meaning* by renowned German psychiatrist Viktor Frankyl. During the Nazi occupation in World War II, Frankyl lost his wife, children, and so many friends to terrible deaths in concentration camps. He witnessed countless horrors, was whipped and beaten, and was somehow spared three times from death. Through it all, he was inspired with a powerful message he felt compelled to share with the world. In essence, it was this belief: *They can take everything they want to take from me,* **but they can't take what I'm thinking**. *I get to choose my thoughts.* This man, who had been through so much, discovered that if he chose to find meaning in any situation, he was able to transform his experience of that situation. And no one could take that away from him! What an amazing thought that no one can control your thinking except *you.*

In the end, as we all know, our bodies are going to die. And our egos are terrified of that fact, because our egos are of the flesh. But physical death is not a concern of the spirit. Our spirits are limitless, and the spirit doesn't worry about the outcome of something. The spirit seeks to live in the grace and the glory of God every day.

No matter what age I am, I know everything comes back to my spirit. I will only be motivated if my spirit and my mind say *Get up!*

If that doesn't happen, my body will sit in this chair all day and not move. Maybe today my body says, *I'm tired, I'm depressed.* My ego says, *I'm losin'.*

Truth is, as I write this, I've had four or five surgeries in the last few years. I *am* tired. My health issues have worn me out. Family problems have worn me out. My business made it through the recession, but I'm worn out!

Each of us has this "worn out" experience in life at some point or another. *But it's what we do with that feeling that makes all the difference.* We can let our minds talk us into giving up. Or we can say "I'm going to get up and *do something*," and our bodies will follow.

I believe the hardest job you'll ever have to do in life is to think. Every day I stop to think about what I want out of this day. How am I going to better myself? What am I going to do to enjoy the day? Even when my physical strength is low, I won't allow my mind to be filled with thoughts of giving up. I know that my God's strength can and will always carry me through. Sure, I'm tired, but my spirit says, *You've got this day to live! Don't waste it.*

My doctor and friends say, "You sure look good. You've got a lot of energy." They see my spirit coming through. They see what happens when I decide I'm going to live this day, because I don't get it back tomorrow.

Not saying it's always easy to live this way. Everything in this book is what I've had to tell myself again and again to be successful in life, to live with appreciation, joy, and gratitude.

Thank you God for what I have...

This is where I have to begin today, and tomorrow, and every day.

Not what I want or what I need...

I'm going to focus on the blessings of this moment, not the desire for something else in the future.

...but what I have.

Living with an attitude of gratitude. That's how I choose to fill the years of my life.

Darol in 2012.

OUT OF THE SHADOW

28

LIVING GENEROUSLY

How giving becomes its own reward

I believe however we've been blessed—financially, spiritually, or maybe with time or wisdom or resources—we all have something to give. But the question is, will we choose to share what we've been given?

When it comes to generosity, I've run across two kinds of people: The tight-fisted person who sees only scarcity, who feels like there's never enough and misses some wonderful opportunities to give; and the open-handed person who sees abundance and shares freely, trusting that their own needs will always be met. The tight-fisted person lives in the shadow, while the open-handed person lives in the light.

Perhaps someone in our past led us to believe that giving is just too risky. We need to protect what we have; don't trust people's motives; don't allow ourselves to be vulnerable. And maybe someone before them did the same. Remember: No matter how many generations have been closed off to generous living, it doesn't have to hold us back from becoming the vessels God created us to be.

For many of us, that means shifting our focus away from money—ridding ourselves of the feeling like we need more and more to feel secure—and beginning to live in a spirit of freedom and generosity. We learn to trust that we'll have all we need, even if we share what we have with others. Whatever it is we have to offer—our time, our money, or even just a touch, a thought, a kind word, or smile—we can all choose to bless someone. In fact, I've found that the more I open my hands to the people around me, the more I receive in my *own* life.

Even as a young kid, I realized this. It's always seemed natural to me to give and not take from the world. One summer in high school I was hired to paint a building downtown. I was sitting outside with my girlfriend on a break one day. This guy comes through town hoboin'. Walks up to us and asks, "Can you spare a dollar or anything?" I looked down at his feet, and his shoes were worn clear through. It just so happened that my mom and dad (Lavon and Ray) had bought me a brand-new pair of shoes that summer— cost $10—which was pretty expensive back in 1961! I didn't think twice. Just went and got those new shoes and handed them to the hobo!

To me, there's nothing like the feeling of being able to give. And I believe giving and receiving are really simultaneous. A lot of people give with the expectation that they'll be given something in the future. But *the joy of sharing comes the second you give. You receive* a gift just as you are giving one! I often hear TV preachers say "Give money to God, and *wait* for the gift!" But I say don't give with the expectation of getting something later! The gift of receiving happens the moment you open your heart. Doesn't matter if it's $1 or $1,000, an hour or a day. The second you give whatever you have, you can feel the joy return to you.

But just as generosity can free our spirits, greed can imprison them. It can destroy people, friendships, and families. Those who live with a tight fist are never satisfied, no matter how much they have. Living in a shadow of insecurity and fear like that can take a toll on relationships.

I often remind people that we all have something

to share. "Just give!" I tell them. "Your heart, your hand, your touch, your love, your look. You may not have a lot of money to give, but you have so many other things. And you have the most important gift of all: *Love*." We can all be vessels on this earth.

Ask yourself today: What resources do I have to offer others—money, time, abilities, blessings? What would it look like for me to truly live an abundant life with an open hand?

29

FORMING A FOUNDATION FOR THE FUTURE

Finding my true calling

Now that I've realized my childhood hope to leave behind the dysfunction and misfortune that marked the shadowy years of my youth, I had to ask myself what was next. I had to figure out how I might use the gifts I've been given, in the years I have left on this earth. From those questions, the *Darol Rodrock Foundation* was born.

On the night of my 70th birthday party, I announced to friends and family what the focus of my remaining years would be. My Foundation exists to be a lifeline for local foster children—especially those who've reached the critical point of aging out of foster care. I think many people are unaware of the great difficulties these children in our communities face.

As I write this, there are more than 6,500 foster children in Kansas alone. The top two reasons they are placed in foster care are abuse/neglect and drug abuse by a parent. While some children are blessed and taken in by families who make a lifelong commitment to love and support them, not all are so fortunate.

Families in Kansas are given approximately $600 a month to care for a foster child. But the day they turn 18, the kids officially "age out" of the system, and the state's money stops coming in. When that happens, it's estimated that 80% of those families ask the kids to leave. Where do they go? They have nothing—no mom, no dad, and no money to take care of themselves. Many of them don't even know how to drive a car.

But it doesn't have to be this way! It is my hope that the Darol Rodrock Foundation—and all the loving hearts who've supported me and my efforts—will help these kids walk out of the shadows of their pasts, so that like me, they can find rich, meaningful lives.

Here are just a few ways the *Darol Rodrock Foundation* has been able to make a difference:

- Working with local caseworkers to provide clothing for children in need.

- Providing essentials for college-bound foster kids, including bedding, towels, toiletries, etc., and sending care packages throughout the year for encouragement.

- Buying sports equipment for those who would love to try out for a sport but don't have the required gear.

- Helping kids with practical life lessons that they didn't learn from their birth parents. For example, we have sponsored classes like "Under the Hood," where they can learn the ins-and-outs of car maintenance, how to fill a gas tank, get a driver's license, insurance information, etc.

- Sharing our resources with other organizations and caring foster families to extend our reach. Recently we were able to help a family take in 5 siblings who would've been split up had they not found a home to stay in together.

And while the Foundation is only a few years old, we've managed to partner with some really exciting names in Kansas City. For three years, we worked with Sporting KC to raise both awareness and to collect donations for local foster-care kids. (Some of you may have seen me flip a coin to start a game and speak at half-time!) Soccer clinics allowed these special kids to visit the Club's official training facility for a three-hour event, including on-field access, a behind-the-scenes tour of the locker room and training areas, group photos with players, autograph signings, and the once-in-a-lifetime opportunity to run drills on the field!

The *Darol Rodrock Foundation* also sponsored Dayton Moore's "C" You In The Major Leagues program, which reaches out to students in underserved areas of the city. Dayton is the Senior Vice President of Baseball Operations and General Manager of the Royals. He started the organization to benefit youth baseball, families in crisis, education, and faith-based programs and organizations.

During the Royals' season, groups of high-school students identified by Dayton Moore's foundation and who need special attention are invited to Kauffman Stadium to watch batting practice and receive a short talk from me and Dayton, followed by a question-and-answer session—all before being treated to dinner and a Royals game! The presentations focus on the "C" qualities of care, character, coach, commitment, competitor, composure, comprehension, concentration, confidence, and courage.

I have spoken several times to some incredible young people through Dayton's program. It was such a great experience for me, getting to meet those great kids and Dayton, who is one of the most charismatic men I've ever met.

I enjoy speaking to kids in the foster-care system. I like to share my story, let them know I've walked in their shoes. I'd like to think it gives them hope, knowing that they don't have to be defined by their past.

And, as I remember well, the holiday season is not a happy time for many of these kids, so we partnered with a local foster organization, Gear Up, to give a few local foster-care children a night to remember. Our first year's event was held on the Country Club Plaza in Kansas City, Mo. Known for its beautiful fountains, statues, shops, and European architecture, the Plaza is spectacular at the holidays—lit by 15 blocks of shining lights.

We took around 100 kids to dinner there and then suggested we go for a walk together to see the sights. It was a cold night, and the Gear Up director said quietly, "Most of these kids don't have coats, Mr. Rodrock." It brought me back to my own childhood, and my heart broke for them.

One moment from that night that's etched in my

memory was when two sisters showed up who'd been separated by the court. Neither knew the other was coming, and they hadn't seen each other in two years. We were all in tears watching that reunion.

And then there was the boy, (a straight-A student, despite all he's been through) who came up to me and pointed to an area nearby. He said, "My dad, sister, and I used to sleep under that bridge over there, Mr. Rodrock." They were homeless, had nothing, and yet this child never gave up.

I gave each of them a $100 bill that night. You should have seen them cry. One little girl said, "My momma has nothing. Even though I don't know her very well, I'm giving my money to her."

Another said, "My little sister wasn't going to have Christmas, but now I'm so happy. I can give her a Christmas this year!"

And another: "I'm buying myself a new coat so maybe next year if we do this again I can go on a walk to see the Plaza lights!"

After that inspiring night, we knew we had to make a holiday tradition for these kids. But we wanted to make it bigger, make it better. So we began our "country Christmas" party for hundreds of foster-care kids. Santa makes an appearance, and kids love going on horse-drawn sleigh rides around the park before sitting down for a good dinner. I always hand out a gift card to each of them, which may be all they receive for Christmas. I have to tell you, I've choked up singing carols with them. Many show up with not even a jacket to wear, so we make sure we always have a collection of winter jackets, hats, gloves, and blankets for them to take.

Kids are filled with so much hope and joy during this special time of year, and we wanted to ensure the circumstances of foster care don't dim that delight for some local kids. Every child should look forward to the holidays. Every child should light up at seeing Santa and eagerly anticipate the surprise waiting inside a brightly wrapped package. To see them rejoice in the Christmas that I never had as a child—that brings me to tears.

I'm excited at the work we've done so far, but there's much more that needs to be accomplished. I have some big plans, which keeps me energized and hopeful for the future!

In truth, this is only the beginning of my hopes for the *Darol Rodrock Foundation.* I hope to someday provide transitional housing for kids aging out of foster care—a safe place for these young people to turn to when they've been turned out by their foster parents. I envision rooms the kids could call their own, a dining hall filled with laughter and family-style meals, full-time and dedicated counselors on duty, and a manager to overlook the "Darol Rodrock Academy."

But my dreams go far beyond just meeting these kids' physical needs! These young people need a safe place in which to grow, a sense of community, guidance, tech training, and services to help them continue their education or get a solid job. And importantly, they need therapy and emotional support so they can begin to leave the shadows of their pasts behind them.

While still in the planning stages, the Darol Rodrock Academy would fill a very real need—one that affects all of us, whether we realize it or not. It's estimated that some 250 children are aging out of foster care in Kansas this year alone. These young people aren't prepared to enter the real world. They're still kids, after all, and most have had terribly difficult and dysfunctional childhoods. Society hasn't provided many fair breaks, and these children are in an uphill battle against poverty, limits to their education, and, for some, the lingering damage of emotional, physical, and sexual abuse.

In fact, according to FosterAdopt Connect, nationally 71% of the girls who age out will have a child out of wedlock before the age of 21. Sadly 74% of boys and 43% of girls will report having a police record. Another 40% will be homeless—because more than half of these young people will find themselves unemployed by age 25. For those that do hold jobs, the majority will not be earning a living wage. Hard to earn a decent wage when 1 in 5 is without a high-school diploma or GED in their mid-20s.

And the way the system is set up, there is little hope in breaking this awful cycle. There is less than a 3% chance for children who have aged out of foster care to earn a college degree at any point in their life, according to the Jim Casey Youth Opportunities Initiative.

I think we must do better by these kids. I understand it's an enormous undertaking. But we *must* do something. With a helping hand, these young people will have a real chance at a *successful life*.

Darol speaking to foster-care youth.

Darol and Dayton Moore speaking to participants of Dayton Moore's "C" You In The Major Leagues program.

*Darol speaking to a crowd of young people in foster care
at Ironwoods Lodge in Kansas.*

Darol with Dayton Moore, the Senior Vice President of Baseball Operations and General Manager of the Royals.

Darol and one of the many foster-care children who was inspired by his personal story and faith in their future.

30

A CALL TO BE THE LIGHT

*Remembering to foster your light
and share it with others*

I've been asked most of my life how I got from there to here. I'm not sure I've answered that question in these pages, but I've made every attempt to pour open my heart and search for it. As painful, quite frankly, as it's been to revisit the past and tell my story, this is how I remember it.

I can only hope my efforts were worthwhile. I pray that my story might inspire someone to walk out of the dark shadow of their past and into the light of

OUT OF THE SHADOW

God, fulfill their purpose, give value to other people, and enrich the world we all live in.

In the end, it comes back to Miss Pinnt. She saw a child desperate for a way out of the darkness, and she opened her heart to me. She shone her love on me and ignited my journey with Jesus, who has walked with me along my path ever since.

And it also comes back to Lavon and Ray. Somehow, they saw that spark of light, and they never gave up on me, even when the shadows of my past threatened to pull me back. Even when I ran away and fought against them, they continued to nurture that light within me, showing me what it was to be loved—unconditionally.

This book has detailed some of the ways I worked in my body, mind and spirit to leave the darkness of my past behind me. And it also highlights the importance of a few key people in the life of Darol. I wouldn't be here today if it wasn't for them. Many friends over the years have loved, encouraged, and supported me. Each person has come into my life at just the right time. And I am truly humbled and appreciative of each of you. It's as if God put you, my dear friends, in my life just when I needed you. And I thank God, and I thank you.

So, in the end, I think my successes came both from my inner drive, the kindness of some very

302

special people, and the powerful words of Jesus. But I can never stop working to continue to live in this light. That's why my sayings have become like daily devotionals to me. In truth, it's a struggle. It can be easy to say, "I got it," and to leave these convictions behind. But my future HAS to be based on the beliefs in this book. I need to keep thinking these things, so that I can keep the shadow of all the pain and ugliness of my past behind me. It's a daily challenge, but it's one I welcome. Because as long as I'm fighting, I know I'm working to stay in the light of Jesus and the light of truth.

I want to encourage anyone who's reading this book to remember, *every day*, to make the choices that put you on the path of freedom from the shadows of your past. To look for the people who are going to encourage and lift you up and help you on that journey. To realize that each new day you have a chance to write your own history. To make it something you'll be proud of.

But more than that, to try to recognize the people around you who are on the same path. And help them. Offer a kind word, lend a hand, share some of your light, and ignite a spark within them, so it can help carry them out of their darkness. Remember: "A candle loses nothing by lighting another candle."

Even by holding this book in your hands, you're

helping! Proceeds from this book help fund the work of the Darol Rodrock Foundation. See? You're already on the right path!

But we would love it if you would consider doing more. Reach out into your community and help a child in need. Or consider helping us in our mission by donating at darolrodrockfoundation.org.

As it says in Ephesians 5:8, "for you were formerly darkness, but now you are Light in the Lord; walk as children of Light."

ACKNOWLEDGEMENTS

When I was told I should write down my story, I had no idea how to begin. But I believe God put certain people in my life at just the right time to make this book happen. What you hold in your hands has been carefully tended to by so many!

I cannot tell you how important Paige was in helping me write this book. Paige is the beautiful daughter of one of my high-school classmates, and she committed herself to writing the book in my words—and filled with my emotions. She taped our conversations for hundreds of hours, and then would devotedly listen to the tapes over and over again to pull out a story that made sense. She is a remarkable person, and I will always know that only Paige could have produced this book in this manner!

I owe special thanks to Judy for pushing me to share my story in the first place, as well as for being an incredible friend and constant support. Without her, none of this would have been possible!

Much thanks goes to my dear friend and fraternity brother Mike for his editing help and unwavering support in the message of this book.

I'm so grateful to Charlotte, Cindy, Katherine, Ty, Danny, Lisa, John, Rachel, and countless others who took the time to read this book in its many forms and provide advice, encouragement, and on occasion, some tough love.

APPENDIX

Young Darol's Moves

YEAR	AGE	TOWN	SITUATION
1944	1-3	Bush City, Kan.	Born in farm house close to Humboldt, Kan., in Grandpa and Grandma Rodrock
1944-51	4 - 7	Iola, Kan.	2nd house on Tennessee Street
1951	7	Winfield, Kan.	Lutheran Children's Orphanage
1951-54	8	Humboldt. Kan.	Grandma & Grandpa Rodrock
1954-55	10	Winfield, Kan.	Lutheran Children's Orphanage
1955-56	11-12	Evening Shade, Ark.	"Uncle" Ray & "Aunt" Mary
1956	12	Coffeyville, Kan.	Summer of '56, back home briefly
1956	12	Trains	Months of riding the rails
1956	12	Kincaid County, Kan. Minkler Star	Uncle Raymond & Aunt Pearline Stephens
1956	12	Seneca, Mo. (school in Wyandotte, Okla.)	Max & sister, Beverly
1956-57	12-13	Kincaid County, Kan.	Lavon & Ray Robinson
1958-59	14-15	Garnett, Kan.	Lavon & Ray Robinson
1960-62	16-18	Marysville, Kan.	Lavon & Ray Robinson
1962	18	Iola, Kan.	Lavon & Ray Robinson
1962	18	Lawrence, Kan.	University of Kansas

Made in the USA
Coppell, TX
20 October 2020

39965766R00184